An RVer's Annual

OTHER BOOKS BY TRAILER LIFE

Full-time RVing: A Complete Guide to Life on the Open Road
Bill and Jan Moeller

The answers to all the questions anyone who dreams of traveling full time in an RV may have can be found in this remarkable new source book. *Full-time RVing* takes the mystery out of fulltiming and makes it possible to fully enjoy this once-in-a-lifetime experience.
$7\frac{1}{4} \times 9\frac{1}{4}$, 352 pages
$14.95 ISBN: 0-934798-14-1

RX for RV Performance & Mileage
John Geraghty and Bill Estes

In 32 chapters, this book covers everything an owner must know about how an engine (particularly a V-8) works, vehicle maintenance, propane and diesel as alternative fuels, eliminating engine "ping," improving exhaust systems and fuel economy, and much more.
$7\frac{3}{4} \times 9\frac{1}{4}$, 359 pages
$14.95 ISBN: 0-934798-08-0

The RV Galley Cookbook
Edited by Beverly Edwards and the editors of *Trailer Life*

Over 250 easy and delicious recipes, including 78 prize-winners from Good Sam Samboree cook-offs around the country. Also contains tips, ideas, and suggestions to help you get the most from your RV galley.
$7\frac{1}{4} \times 9\frac{1}{4}$, 252 pages
$14.95 ISBN: 0-934798-17-6

COMING SOON—Watch for our announcements in your mail—The all-new comprehensive travel series, *RVing America's Backroads* and a completely revised up-to-date version of *Trailer Life's RV Repair and Maintenance Manual.*

These books are available at fine bookstores everywhere. Or, you may order directly from Trailer Life. For each book ordered, simply send us the name of the book, the price, plus $2 per book for shipping and handling (California residents please add $6\frac{1}{2}$% sales tax). Mail to:

Trailer Life Books, PO Box 4500, Agoura, CA 91301

You may call our Customer Service representatives if you wish to charge your order or if you want more information. Phone, toll-free, Monday through Friday, 7:00 A.M. to 6:00 P.M.; Saturday, 7:30 A.M. to 12:30 P.M. Pacific Time, **1-800-234-3450.**

An RVer's Annual

The Best of Trailer Life and MotorHome

Edited by
Rena Copperman

Trailer Life Books
Agoura, California

Trailer Life Book Division

President: **Richard Rouse**
Vice President/General Manager: **Ted Binder**
Vice President/Publisher, Book Division: **Michael Schneider**
General Manager, Book Division: **Rena Copperman**
Assistant Manager, Book Division: **Cindy Lang**

First Edition

Printed in the United States of America
5 4 3 2 1

Cover design: **Mirante Almazan**
Cover photograph: **Bill Gleasner**
Interior design: **Mirante Almazan**
Production manager: **Rena Copperman**
Editorial assistant: **Judi Lazarus**
Indexer: **Barbara Wurf**
Contents map: **Robert Lamarche**

This book was set in ITC Aster by
Publisher's Typography
and printed on 60-pound Sterling Web Gloss
with a 12-point Carolina cover by
R.R. Donnelley and Sons in Willard, Ohio.

ISSN 1040–3744

ISBN 0–934798–21–4

Contents

TRA

57 **Colter Country**
Glenn and Maxine Bamburg

53 **Stepping High**
Fred and Dora Burris

38 **Superior Playground**
Robert J. and Geraldine R. Smi

70 **A Slice in Time**
Jan Gumpecht Bannan

64 **Stone Rainbows**
Glenn and Maxine Bamburg

76 **California Suite**
Doug Emerson

97 **Return to Espíritu**
Emil Barjak

84 **The Baja Experience**
Fred Hoctor

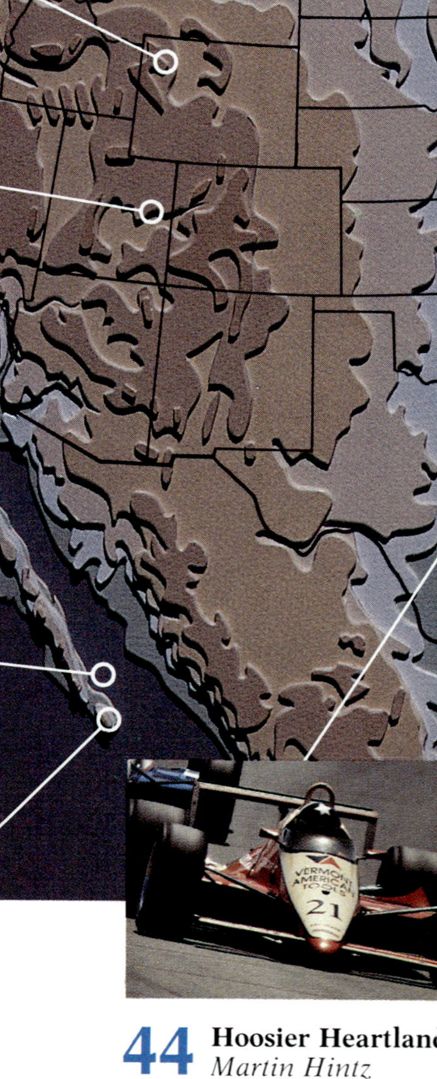

44 **Hoosier Heartlan**
Martin Hintz

VEL

24 **Fall Hopping in the Finger Lakes**
Patricia L. Barnes

5 **Drop Anchor in Acadia**
Robert J. Smith

19 **Massachusetts Marvels**
Myrna L. and Gerald F. Courtney

11 **Wonderful West Virginia**
Mary Cobb

102 **Counties Cork and Kerry**
Michael Vernon

30 **Creole Nature Trail**
Peter M. Lewis

Special Features

111 **Dollars and Sense**
Dick Gould

113 **Automatic Teller Machines**
Sherry McBride

115 **Flea for All**
Barbara Leonard

121 **Cinder Fever**
C.J. Burkhart

Personalities

131 **In Search of Quail**
Tom Huggler

136 **Fishing for Dollars**
Jim Zumbo

140 **Our Season in the Sun**
Bill Poss

Technical

151 **The Energy Source (Batteries)**
Brian Robertson

157 **Brake Systems**
Brian Robertson

163 **Play It Cool (Cooling Systems)**
Brian Robertson

The Constitution

171 **Celebrating the Constitution**
Barbara Leonard

176 **Philadelphia**
Robert J. Smith

181 **Valley Forge**
Robert J. and Geraldine R. Smith

184 **The First State**
Bill and Bert Schill

189 **Index**

PHOTO: JIM VINCENT

FOREWORD

Among the many attractive aspects of RV travel, independence is among the most compelling. Anyone who has sampled the wide variety of RV travel destinations probably has recognized the unique feeling that results from having an extension of one's own residence along for the trip.

Thus, anyone who already knows even a little about RVs and loves to travel probably will come down with a serious case of wanderlust after reading this book. It is a collection of stories about some of the most scenic and interesting destinations in this country—only a sampling, however, because it was extracted from one year of our two highly regarded magazines, *Trailer Life* and *MotorHome.* Not even magazines as specifically focused on RV travel as these can do justice to the world of travel in one year. But I trust this volume will give you the essence of why we have become such addicts to the RV way of life.

This book is your passport to adventure—offering special insight into a fascinating variety of travel destinations. For example, everyone has heard of Yellowstone National Park (*see* "Coulter Country," page 57). But not everyone knows of the role mountain man John Colter played in the early 1800s in determining the future of the areas now known as Yellowstone and Grand Teton national parks. Seeing these magnificent areas is exciting enough; imagining how John Colter might have felt about them in 1808 adds a very special new dimension.

In addition, we have included a variety of other material, including some technical self-help articles that should be of practical use.

From Maine to Mexico, story after story in this book will set your mind wandering as you place yourself in the magnificent and colorful scenes presented here. If you become infected, you're invited to blame us. We planned it that way!

Bill Estes
Associate Publisher
Trailer Life and *MotorHome*

PREFACE

The task of choosing the best features from the pages of *Trailer Life* and *MotorHome* magazines has been a difficult one. Over the past year hundreds of excellent travel stories, personality pieces, and technical articles have appeared in the publications, acknowledged as the most outstanding in their field. Where does one begin?

I started by consulting with the publishers and editors of the two magazines. Naturally, each one had a favorite or two—and each one was different! I reread the past year's issues and decided that I would select the ones that lingered most in the memory, provided special information, or just pure pleasure. The travel articles were chosen to represent a cross-section of our country: East, South, North, Central, and West. The special features provided useful information *(Dollars and Sense, Flea for All)*, or shared a special interest with us *(Cinder Fever)*. Tom Huggler *(In Search of Quail)*, Bill and Kate Poss *(Our Season in the Sun)*, and Jim Zumbo *(Fishing for Dollars)* epitomize the free spirit of the RVer. And none of us will forget the 200th anniversary of our nation's Constitution: *Trailer Life*'s notable feature preserves some of these memories for us.

A special thanks to the staffs of *Trailer Life* and *MotorHome* magazines: Bill Estes, Barbara Leonard, Bob Livingston, Sherry McBride, Yvonne Vollert, Gail Harrington, Glenn Hamaguchi, Jeanne Jones, and Susie Lieu. They are editors, authors, and artists without peer: their good sense, thoroughgoing knowledge, and basic understanding of their crafts and their commitment to excellence mark every page of this book.

"Of journeying, the benefits are many: the freshness it brings to the heart, the seeing and rehearing of marvelous things, the delight of beholding cities, the meeting of unknown friends. . . ." (Sa'dī [1184–1291]). We hope this collection will enhance *your* journeying.

RENA COPPERMAN
Editor

Travel

THE EAST

Drop Anchor in Acadia

Maine's Mount Desert Island is the center of an archipelago of unequaled wild grandeur

Robert J. Smith

If you are looking for the best of the rock-bound coast of Maine, anchor your RV on Mount Desert Island, the site of Acadia National Park and the center of an archipelago whose wild grandeur is unequaled elsewhere in the United States.

Mount Desert Island, a geologic wonder, was fashioned when ice-age glaciers carved an existing mountain into a labyrinth of valleys, depressions, fjord-like inlets, peninsulas and stony headlands, whose broad bastions shatter huge waves, breaking them into harmless flying spume. Nature has added lakes and ponds and cloaked the whole in forests of fir and spruce, hemlock and pine. Man also has lent a hand with numerous historic sites, elegant homes, gracious inns, superb restaurants, excellent antique and curio shops, and much, much more. Knowledgeable travelers agree that the Acadia area is the best of Maine.

PHOTO: ROBERT J. SMITH

Sunsets in the Mount Desert area are often spectacular; this one is a view of Southwest Harbour.

Acadia National Park, the hub of this scenic wonderland, covers 22 square miles of Mount Desert Island, part of Schoodic Peninsula and part of the small Isle au Haut. There are two campgrounds inside the park and several private campgrounds near the park's perimeter. Con-

PHOTO: ROBERT J. SMITH

sult your *1989 Trailer Life Campground & RV Services Directory* for complete listings. Excellent roads thread their way around the area's bays and inlets, climb mountains, pierce forests and, in general, make the area ideal for RVers.

At the park's visitors center, we viewed an excellent educational film, picked up maps and brochures, and rented a self-guiding tape tour. We found that sightseeing in the park can be as fast or as leisurely as one wishes. A 20-mile loop road, starting at the visitors center, touches many of the park's finest features. Along the drive, which has many viewpoints, you'll see glacier-carved valleys, surf-pounded cliffs, lakes and a rocky shoreline. The road passes interesting places such as Thunder Hole, which lives up to its name when waves crash into caverns below; Otter Point, where colorful buoys mark lobster traps; and Jordon Pond House, where generations of visitors have enjoyed midafternoon tea and popovers. A side road climbs to the crest of Cadillac Mountain, the highest point on our Atlantic Coast and the point where panoramic views stretch in every direction. The loop road returns through sylvan terrain to the visitors center.

PHOTO: ROBERT J. SMITH

For a leisurely inspection of the park, there are many trails and carriage paths, some of which are open to cyclists and horseback riders. Along the coast, you can inspect tidepools or swim, if icy water is not a deterrent. A well-rounded program of nature hikes with park rangers makes the experience more enjoyable. But, however you explore it, this park impresses.

Other roads skirting the park's perimeter pass the only fjord on the East Coast and lead to picturesque harbors where sailboats, tied up to pink buoys, look like dabs of white paint on a cerulean canvas, and their colorful dinghies shuttle from ship to shore like busy water bugs. Every harbor has its quota of curio and antique shops, where you can find everything from lobster buoys to Chippendale furniture. Lobster pounds abound, and you can gorge on Maine's superb decapode crustaceans for a modest price. We watched the cooks haul steaming baskets of the red beauties from their outdoor cookers and inhaled the unmistakable aroma. The huge piles of wood, stacked and ready to feed the cooking fires, testify to the popularity of this form of diet busting.

Bar Harbor, one of the East Coast's world-famous resort towns, is the island's main settlement. However, during the height of the summer season, its streets get as crowded as a carnival midway. Even so, shoppers and gourmets are more than happy with its offerings.

Ellsworth, the largest town in the area and gateway to the national park, has many gracious old homes, as does much of this area of Maine. Their numbers are surprising, but Down Easters have a reputation for protecting their architectural heritage. We sensed that these semihistoric structures were as much a part of the landscape as the rocky ground beneath their foundations. Their presence gives the area a feeling of stability and longevity.

Colorful rowboats tied up to a pier make colorful photographs.

A drive around the Blue Hill Peninsula revealed more primitive coastal beauty. The road skirts lovely Blue Hill Bay, then cuts westward to span Eggemoggin Reach to Deer Isle, the home of the picturesque fishing village of Stonington. This is the place to watch fishermen going about their everyday tasks.

Castine, a colorful town at the mouth of the Penobscot River, was first established by the Plymouth Pilgrims. At different times it has been held by the French, Dutch, British and American Revolutionists. One of the worst naval losses in American history occurred when the Continentals lost more than 36 ships as they attempted to wrest Castine from the British. We found the town's 100-plus historical markers the key to its tumultuous past. Many of its old homes date to the 1800s, and a number of them were built in the late 1700s. One, the John Perkins House, was built before the Revolution. (Guided tours are offered Wednesdays and Sundays 2 P.M. and 5 P.M. during July and August.)

Castine is the home of the Maine Maritime Academy and also the home port for the academy's huge, seagoing training ship, the *State of Maine*. When the ship is in port, usually after July 1, it is open for free guided tours.

At Bucksport we discovered a genuine Maine landmark, the Jed Prouty Inn. The inn, built in 1798 as a stagecoach stop, has played host to such notables as Daniel Webster and Jefferson Davis, as well as U.S. Presidents Martin Van Buren, Andrew Jackson and William Henry Harrison. As we walked into the inn, we felt as if we were rubbing elbows with some very important ghosts.

We were eager to see Fort Knox. We had heard that this National Historic Landmark was a stunning example of military architecture—and so it is. This superb fortification, built on a bend in the Penobscot River, across from Bucksport, guarded the 32-mile section of the river between Castine and Bangor. Its huge granite blocks were so perfectly cut and fitted that their joints are almost imperceptible. Although its battlements appear impregnable, it has never been tested.

Another of our outings took us northward, along U.S. Highway 1, to the Canadian province of New Brunswick. Here we visited Roosevelt Campobello International Park. The main feature of the park is the 34-room "cottage" that was President Franklin Delano Roosevelt's favorite summer haven. FDR started coming here at the age of one in 1883, and returned yearly until he was stricken by polio in 1921. He returned in 1933 after the first 100 days of his presidency, and also visited in 1936 and 1939. It was easy for us to imagine a handicapped president, sitting before the large window in the living room, gazing longingly over Passamaquoddy Bay and reliving the days when he sailed its waters with joyous abandon.

Most of the rooms are small. The furnishings, many of them used by the Roosevelts, are simple—even Spartan—with wicker predominating. Personal items such as a collection of canes, telescope, crib and phon-

PHOTO: ROBERT J. SMITH

One of dozens of curio shops on Mount Desert Island features lobster trap buoys hanging outside.

ograph are on view including a large megaphone used by Eleanor Roosevelt to call the children for meals or chores.

New Brunswick has a park with trailer sites at nearby Herring Cove. There are other campgrounds in nearby Lubec, Maine. Campobello International Park is open the Saturday before Memorial Day and remains open for 20 weeks. Visiting hours are 9 A.M. to 5 P.M.; admission is free.

On our return, we stopped at West Quoddy Head Light, which sits on the most easterly point of land in the nation. The candy-striped lighthouse is a popular photo subject, but we ran into a common bugaboo—it was being painted, and the scaffolding ruined picture possibilities.

Along the route, the piles of rocks and rock fences attested to the grim reality of farming in Maine, as do the barns connected to homes by enclosed walkways. Huge woodpiles forecasted a long winter to come. Such signs help one understand why this area breeds people as tough and enduring as the state's rocky underpinning.

We found the area so exciting that we plan to return the next time we travel east of the Mississippi River. If you happen to be in the area, drop your RV anchor at Acadia and start enjoying some of the best sightseeing in America.

Wonderful West Virginia

Water sports and breathtaking panoramas make the southeastern section of the Mountain State a treasure trove for travelers

Mary Cobb

PHOTO: GERALD S. RATLIFF

Authentically dressed "Colonials" stroll the grounds of the General Lewis Inn in Lewisburg.

If you're looking for someplace new to explore in the United States, a kite-shaped section of southeastern West Virginia is just waiting for you and your motorhome!

Take a ruler, a pencil and a map of the Mountain State, and draw a straight line from Princeton at the southern terminus of the West Virginia Turnpike (Interstate 77), northeast to White Sulphur Springs, northwest to Hico on U.S. Highway 60, south to Beckley, and back to Princeton. You've just enclosed an area that offers you water sports, unusual sightseeing and breathtaking mountain panoramas.

For your West Virginia visit, you may want to make your home base at Pipestem Resort State Park. The park is located 20 miles north of Princeton and 12 miles south of Hinton on State Highway 20. The Athens Road exit on Interstate 77 will bring you within 14 miles of the park.

Often referred to as the crown jewel in West Virginia's fine park system, Pipestem is named for the hollow-stemmed shrub that grows in the area and was used by Indians and settlers as stems for their pipes.

The 4,023-acre park is located in a pastoral setting of rolling green fields, edged by picturesque, split-rail fences. One of the most attractive sections of the park, about midway between the entrance and the main lodge, is reserved for recreational vehicles. Secluded in groves of oak, poplar and hickory trees are 50 sites. All hookups are provided at 31 of the spaces, electric only at 19. Playground equipment, bathhouse and

PHOTO: GERALD S. RATLIFF

White-water rafting trip takes rafters under the New River Gorge Bridge.

laundry are conveniently located within the campground.

During the height of the season, from Memorial Day to Labor Day, 25 spaces are reserved and 25 are on a first-come basis; from Labor Day to Memorial Day, all spaces are on a first-come basis.

Once you're settled, you may wonder if there really are attractions worth exploring outside this idyllic park! From magnificent vistas and cool hiking trails to a challenging golf course and canyon tram, the park was planned as a family vacation spot.

Filigreed shadows cast from white oak and white pine trees play on the rolling fairways of Pipestem's 18-hole championship golf course. Designed by well-known golf-course architect Geoffrey Cornish, the classic course blends so subtly into the natural beauty of the mountaintop that one might think it came into being through natural creation, rather than through man-made development.

The park also has a nine-hole, par-3 course; a miniature-golf course; a driving range; tennis courts; archery and cycling facilities; indoor and outdoor swimming pools; horseback riding and overnight pilgrimages; a well-stocked 16-acre lake with paddleboats; a licensed day-care center for tots; an observation tower with a spectacular view of the park; and an amphitheater where live entertainment is provided in summer.

A full-time naturalist conducts nature walks and evening programs at the park's Nature Center. More than 400 species of wildflowers and 168 species of birds, including the golden eagle, have been sighted here.

The resort's seven-level lodge overlooks a deep gorge, which confines the winding Bluestone River. Rocks beneath the surface of the water appear to have a bluish cast, thus the name. A 3,600-foot aerial tram carries visitors from the park's main complex, elevation 2,639 feet, into the gorge, where a second lodge is located. If you look closely during the 6½-minute trip down the mountain, you can see the remains of a moonshine still, discovered when the tram was installed. In the early 1900s, stills were common here in "corn-likker country."

During the summer season, craftspeople work in the Visitors Center, which serves as the tram's upper terminal. Quality West Virginia crafts may be purchased, or guests may simply browse and observe the craftspeople at work.

If RV guests want to enjoy a night out, they can dine in the restaurant at the main lodge and enjoy sweeping views of the Allegheny Mountains, crowned with the brilliant glow of the setting sun, or they can sample

PHOTO: GERALD S. RATLIFF

Scenes like this in southeastern West Virginia live up to the state's motto: Almost Heaven.

country cooking at its best in the Mountain Creek Lodge dining room in the gorge.

There's more to see and do in southeastern West Virginia—if you can bear to leave this mountain paradise. Water enthusiasts will find this part of the state lives up to its tourism slogan, "Almost Heaven." Eight miles north of Pipestem, on State Highway 20, is Bluestone State Park, which overlooks Bluestone Lake, 1,800 acres of clear, water encircled by densely forested mountains. Boats, skiing and fishing equipment can be obtained at the docks. For those who prefers more rugged recreation, 20,000 acres of wilderness at the Bluestone Public Hunting and Fishing Area are adjacent to the park.

The New, Greenbrier and Bluestone rivers, which converge at Hinton—once a busy railroad center—are alive with walleye, smallmouth and rock bass, and channel and flathead catfish. Trout streams also are plentiful in southeastern West Virginia. If you're lucky, you may hook a hard-fighting golden trout, a fish that was developed in the Mountain State in 1954. Glinting in the sun like a newly minted gold piece, this catch will match wits with any experienced fisherman.

About 10 miles north of Hinton in the New River is awesome Sandstone Falls, one of the best fishing spots in the state. Fishermen can reach the falls by taking the River Road on the Raleigh County side of the New River, opposite Hinton in Summers County.

Not to be missed while you are in West Virginia is an exciting whitewater trip on the New River. There are many excellent rafting companies in the vicinity of the rapid-laced river, most headquartered between Hico and Glen Jean.

The New River is actually the oldest river on the North American continent, tracing its lineage to the ancient Teays River System, which covered a large portion of central North America 100 million years ago. Declared a national river by Congress in 1978, the New is being preserved as much as possible in its natural state, along with 62,000 acres of land within its designated boundaries.

Thundering rapids and powerful hydraulics in the river will toss your raft effortlessly about, fiercely battling you for its control. Between the rapids, however, are quiet pools of water where you can relax and listen to your guides spin stories of the New River. At the turn of the century, the canyon was dotted with towns inhabited by people who worked in the prosperous mining and timbering industries along the river. Hundreds of thousands of dollars of business passed through the canyon's bustling commercial center, the little town of Thurmond. This town also was the weekend destination of the hard-working miners and lumberjacks who came looking for fun and excitement—and if they didn't find what they were looking for, they created it!

One of the many legends of this era is about a poker game that continued for 14 years, day and night, at a grand hotel in the canyon. The players changed, but the game never stopped. Alcohol and money were plentiful in those days, and few weekends passed without numerous brawls and a shoot-out or two, according to handed-down stories.

Near the end of your white-water trip, you will pass under the spectacular New River Gorge Bridge, which provides the vital link in the corridor that connects Interstate 79 and Interstate 77. The bridge, completed in 1977, has the longest steel arch in the world—a span of 1,700 feet with a rise of 360 feet. From end to end, the bridge is 3,030 feet long and stands 876 feet above the New River.

PHOTO: GERALD S. RATLIFF

This old grist mill at Babcock State Park is a favorite spot for taking pictures.

So fascinated have people been with this engineering masterpiece that one side of the bridge is closed to traffic on the second Saturday in October each year, allowing pedestrians to safely walk its length and experience the unobstructed grandeur of the canyon. Called Bridge Day, the event has become a major West Virginia festival, with musical entertainment, contests, arts and crafts, and plenty of good food.

Unless you are prepared to stay several weeks, it is impossible to see all the interesting attractions in this part of the state in one visit.

There are, for example, several state parks, each with its own particular charm. At Babcock State Park, on State Highway 41 near Clifftop, you will find an operating grist mill where visitors can purchase freshly ground cornmeal and buckwheat flour.

At Grandview State Park, on State Highway 307, off U.S. 19 south of Beckley, you can enjoy outdoor drama at its finest in the Cliffside Amphitheatre. Under a canopy of stars, surrounded by acres of the state flower, the great rhododendron, the birth and early history of West Virginia unfold in *Honey in the Rock*, and the historic feud between the Hatfields and McCoys is retold.

In Beckley's New River Park is an Exhibition Coal Mine, once a working mine. Visitors ride in remodeled coal cars through 1,500 feet of underground passageways where, years ago, men labored in narrow tunnels flat on their backs. A museum next to the mine traces the history of mining, a major West Virginia industry, through pictures and artifacts.

Should you be in West Virginia during the last full weekend in August, you'll want to take in one of the state's largest exhibits, the Appalachian Arts and Crafts Festival. This popular festival is held in Beckley at the Raleigh County Armory, Civic Center.

Springs of sulphur water, once believed to cure just about any ailment, are scattered throughout this part of the state. People traveled from miles around "to take the waters," and a number of resorts were built more than a century ago to accommodate these visitors. A gala social whirl at the spas enabled the "right" young ladies to meet the "right" young men, while their elders endured their mineral-water treatments, apparently oblivious to the fact that the odor wafting from their tonic baths was akin to that of rotten eggs.

One of these stately resorts was The Greenbrier at White Sulphur Springs, a world-renowned hostelry today. Here the Duke and Dutchess of Windsor waltzed the night away, President Dwight D. Eisenhower played many a round of golf, and names like Astor, du Pont, Kennedy and Vanderbilt dotted the register through the years.

Apart from being a playground for the wealthy and titled, The Greenbrier has other reasons for its unique place in the history of West Virginia. During World War II, the resort served as an internment center for foreign diplomats and later as a U.S. Army hospital where 20,000 soldiers were treated.

After the war, The Greenbrier underwent extensive renovation and was completely and lavishly redecorated by internationally recognized interior decorator Dorothy Draper. Soon this beautiful 6,500-acre spa regained its lofty position as one of the country's most elegant resorts. Tours of The Greenbrier can be arranged by calling the resort's social director.

While in White Sulphur Springs, you may want to stop by the Federal Fish Hatchery, where you can see brook, rainbow and brown trout in various states of development. Also in the town is an unusual house, publicized as the only inhabited house in the world made from coal. This modern, six-room private residence was built in 1959 with blocks of cannel coal, cemented with black mortar and glazed for waterproofing. The house is not open to the public, but a similar coal structure next door houses a gift shop where coal jewelry and West Virginia crafts can be purchased.

It would not be cricket, even for RVers, to visit West Virginia without visiting some of the state's country inns. Just half a mile from the entrance to Pipestem is The Oak Supper Club, where a yellow ribbon tied around a giant oak tree warmly welcomes you. A local reporter once wrote of his meal at this inn, "While the spareribs were 'almost heaven,' the chicken pushed the dish right on into the promised land!"

At Pence Springs, on State Highway 3, is the delightful Riverside Inn, a rustic inn restored as an English roadside tavern. English country dishes, including such delectable fare as colonial game pie and fruit-stuffed duckling, are brought to your table by costumed servers. You can dine on the porch if you like, your meal complemented by an orchestra of nighttime creatures and the rhythmic flow of the nearby Greenbrier River. To complete your visit, the proprietor will share with you the story of the inn's mysterious resident ghost.

At the General Lewis Inn in Lewisburg, guests not only can have a delightful meal, but antique buffs in the family will be treated to a trip down Memory Hall, long hallways lined with artifacts of yesteryear. All the rooms in this aristocratic old inn are furnished with antiques, and one section of the inn dates back to 1834.

In another part of Lewisburg is Fort Savannah Inn, whose musical name is the Indian word for "grassy plateau." The inn was built on the site of an early American fort and probably is a reasonable facsimile. It was from here that General Andrew Lewis mustered his forces in the fall of 1774 for the march to Point Pleasant, where he would defeat

Shawnee Chief Cornstalk, an encounter often referred to as the first battle of the American Revolution.

The most revered historic site in Lewisburg is the Old Stone Church, built by Presbyterian settlers in 1796. Years of devoted care have kept the box-shaped building, constructed of native limestone, in excellent condition. It's the oldest unrestored church in continuous use west of the Allegheny Mountains.

Long-handled collection boxes, made in 1844 by a member of the congregation and a 1611 first edition of the King James Bible can be seen in the vestibule.

Family spelunkers will want to explore West Virginia's subterranean wonderland—Organ Cave on U.S. 19, three miles south of Ronceverte, and Lost World Caverns near Lewisburg. Organ Cave, third largest cave in the United States, was named for its 40-foot limestone columns, which resemble pipes of an organ and, when struck, produce sounds not unlike musical strains. Because the cave was rich in saltpeter, an ingredient used to make gunpowder, it served as an arsenal during the Civil War for General Robert E. Lee. The general himself is immortalized by his unmistakable likeness in a natural bust of limestone.

In the strangely beautiful Lost World Caverns, you will walk on a prehistoric ocean floor and touch towering stalagmites formed over millions of years. The main cave is a 1,000-foot-long single room containing several waterfalls. The mystery of the endless caverns will be limited only by your imagination as you enter the Crystal Palace, Grotto of Venus, Grand Canyon and Petrified Forest.

You may be the first of your friends to discover this small but delightful section of southeastern West Virginia, but among RVers, travel treasures are to be shared. Once you've been here, you can be sure your friends won't be far behind!

Additional Information

Fishing:
Division of Wildlife Resources
Department of Natural Resources
State of West Virginia
State Capitol
Charleston, West Virginia 25305

Travel:
Travel Division
Department of Commerce
State of West Virginia
State Capitol
Charleston, West Virginia 25305
(800) Call WVA (toll-free)
(Re: white-water rafting companies, country inns, caves, state parks, events)

Accommodations:
Pipestem Resort State Park
Pipestem, West Virginia 25979
(304) 466-1800

The Greenbrier
White Sulphur Springs,
West Virginia 24986
(304) 536-1110 or toll-free outside West Virginia: (800) 624-6070.

Massachusetts Marvels

Pumpkins, cranberry relish, scarecrows, and whirlygigs—they're all part of this state's autumn magic

Myrna L. and Gerald F. Courtney

If it's red, orange and gold, smells like apple cider and hickory smoke, and gives you an irresistible urge to run about in piles of dry leaves, then it must be Massachusetts in the fall. If you are including this unique state as just one area you'll be RVing through for a fall foliage tour, you'll probably have to concentrate your activities a little, which may be the most difficult part of your trip, since the wonderful fall color is just the beginning of the marvels to be found in Massachusetts.

There's something here for everyone's interests: People with a penchant for the past will find themselves in history heaven in Massachusetts, where our nation began more than 300 years ago. Visiting scholars have only to wander around Harvard Square to get an academic rush that will boggle the mind. Fishermen can replenish their tall tales' supply to last through a whole generation of campfire sessions. And the sports enthusiast can start at Fenway Park or the National Basketball Hall of Fame.

As for RVers, we can visit Massachusetts with all this in mind, but thousands of us come each year as blatant leaf-peekers. We flock to see the incredible color that has tempted the muses of Frost, Thoreau, Longfellow, Hawthorne and many others, past and present. The quaint country roads become bumper-to-bumper passages from one golden hillside to the next leaf-littered village common. Yes, there are crowds, and yes, there are traffic jams sometimes. But, ah, my fellow RVers, it's worth every minute!

And there are ways to avoid congested roads. Once we sat in discouraging traffic after a day of wandering through those gorgeous backwoods roads. Instead of ruining our day with complaints about traffic, we used the CB radio to ask if anyone knew a nice place for dinner. Back

Top, ***Thousands of RVers visit Massachusetts every year during the height of the leaf-peeking season.*** **Bottom,** ***This Rockport fishing shack, called Motif No. 1, is the most frequently painted subject of local artists.***

came a jolly voice suggesting we pull out of traffic and go back to an inn we had passed. We did and then sat in front of a cozy fire and a window with the best view of the foliage-covered hills we had had all day, while enjoying a lovely meal. When we were ready to head back to the campground, the roads were once again obligingly easy to handle.

PHOTO: DON MAGARY

Like the nature-wise squirrels, native New Englanders use the fall season as a preparatory time for winter. In the midst of the ever-changing splendor, they may be cleaning up, stockpiling or battening down. Or maybe those empty shops and closed campgrounds you may encounter later in the season simply testify to the owners' good sense in deciding to go out and enjoy this miracle of nature themselves! In any case, it's a wise RVer who plans ahead and makes sure campgrounds are open through his stay, especially after mid-October.

PHOTO: GERALD F. COURTNEY

Near Boston there are several campgrounds that operate year-round, including Normandy Farms in Foxboro, and Boston Hub KOA in Wrentham, which is open into November. To be sure they're open, check your *1989 Trailer Life Campground & RV Services Directory.*

Normandy Farms Campground provides tours of Boston, which can save you some driving headaches in our nation's seventh-largest city. The campground is located smack-dab in the middle of some of the finest fall foliage and pines to be found. Small towns and villages nearby provide atmosphere for long, leisurely hours of browsing and driving around to do what you came for, leaf-peeking! The roadside stands welcome you with apple pie and cider. There are homemade jellies and cranberry relish and fields of pumpkins for the choosing. New England is justifiably famous for handcrafted items, and every town holds craft bazaars and fairs throughout the fall. If you can take your eyes off the brilliance of the foliage as you drive, you'll find many cozy shops and barns where you can admire straw wreaths and stuffed dolls, "whirlygigs" to tell you which way the wind blows, fine woodworking, needlework and hand-blown glass. For local craft events, check flyers posted in grocery stores and on campground bulletin boards. An excellent guidebook, *Handcraft Centers of New England,* is available for about $8 from the Crafts Editor, Yankee Books, Main Street, Dublin, New Hampshire 03444.

PHOTO: GREG L. RYAN

Reds and golds and browns are at their best on sunny days, although you'll experience some rain and drizzle too, most likely. Do plan to be out and about just before sunset. There is something special about the color of the leaves when the low sun is slanting through the trees. There is a certain translucence, a kind of radiance, that brightens the countryside. Find a spot to park beside the road to watch the magic happen.

Quaking aspens literally quake in the breeze, hence their name. Sugar maples are tapped each spring for sugary sap.

If you find yourself in some small village about dinnertime, check locally (again, grocery stores are a good bet) for announcements of church suppers. New England is famous for church suppers, and you'll see why if you happen on one. For a surprisingly small cost, you'll be treated to roast turkey and pumpkin pie or baked beans and ham with all the trimmings, enjoyed in the company of friendly townsfolk. Often the suppers are in conjunction with a craft fair, some of which are very worthwhile. Some of the best-known suppers require reservations.

Boston, of course, is one of those cities of the world in which it takes weeks to see everything. High on your must-see list is the Freedom Trail, which can be started at Faneuil Hall, where statesmen gathered during the Revolution. From here, you can follow well-marked signs and a red line on the sidewalk through some of the most famous sites in history, including Paul Revere's home and the Old North Church, where his lantern signaled the coming of the British. Stop at the information center at Lafayette Mall on the common, Tremont Street, or the visitors center at 15 State Street, which is run by the National Park Service.

Quincy Market, next to Faneuil Hall, is a riot of shops and food stalls unequalled in the state. There's fresh produce, too. If you are not tempted by the Indian pudding or lobster at Quincy Market, you might be in the mood for Durgin Park in North Market. There you'll be insulted by waitresses who have been bullying satisfied customers for generations while serving up some of the most famed food in New England. For further information about Boston, call the Convention and Visitors Bureau at (617) 536-4100.

Perhaps one of the most stirring moments of your trip will be when you first see the statue of the Minuteman in Concord or the Lexington Battle Green, where the first conflict of the Revolutionary War took place. Sit in the tavern where farmers and merchants argued about revolution, or see the plaque commemorating where a soldier died on his own front steps, and you'll experience an unforgettable history lesson.

A pleasant way to spend a fall afternoon is sitting on the banks of the Charles River to watch the Charles Regatta, the world's largest sculling competition. In October you'll be among about 100,000 people who come to watch 4,000 participants from Harvard and other colleges. Scullers "bend to the wind" in rowing teams of four or eight, while picnickers line the banks and cheer favorites. Complete with tents and balloons and crisp fall air, it's an exciting event. Call (617) 727-9547 for more details.

Other areas of Massachusetts you'll want to include are Plimoth Plantation and Sturbridge Village, both living museums. Plimoth Plantation is an authentically reconstructed hamlet of 1627, with costumed people representing the Pilgrims who landed there on the *Mayflower* and survived the first horrible winter of 1620. The "villagers" will not even speak out of character.

PHOTOS: GERALD F. COURTNEY

Top, *Fall brings its own special splendor to the Massachusetts countryside; no one is exempt from taking it—or raking it—all in.* Bottom, *Plimoth Plantation and Sturbridge Village remain living museums of the Puritans and the Pilgrims.*

One beribboned and becapped matron was asked about Thanksgiving. "Thanksgiving?" she replied. What do you mean? "I don't know about such a day." Of course, Thanksgiving hadn't been invented yet! When asked if "they" had books to read, she sniffed haughtily in her best Puritan style and replied, "They? If you mean *we,* mum, indeed, Captain Standish has a Bible!"

Plimoth has an outstanding November program re-creating the first Thanksgiving, which is open to the public. Also you can tour the *Mayflower II* and see Plymouth Rock itself. For information, contact Plimoth Plantation, Box 1620, Plymouth, Massachusetts 02360; (617) 746-1622.

Near Plymouth is Cranberry World Visitors Center at 225 Water Street. Here are cranberry bogs, a model of a cranberry farm, cooking demonstrations and free refreshments. Admission is free.

Sturbridge Village is a place of wonder on a crisp fall day. This setting brings the 1800s to life. Two hundred acres are devoted to life exactly as it was for our forefathers, with a working farm and shops and the atmospheric old Bullard Tavern. You may encounter a black-cloaked woman hurrying to church, ask the printer for a flyer he's working on, or help gather pumpkins and squash. Wear good shoes and spend the day walking through the 40 restored buildings under the maple trees. Sturbridge Village is a showplace for crafts, and you can observe the making of punched-tin lanterns, straw brooms and wooden barrels, which you can also purchase in the gift shop. You can participate in the activities by preparing your own meal, from chopping the wood to cooking over an open hearth. Some activities require advance reservations. Before your visit, request a list of scheduled events from Old Sturbridge Village, 1 Old Sturbridge Village Road, Sturbridge, Mass. 01566-0200; (617) 347-3362. There are campgrounds nearby, but be sure to check your directory for months of operation; some close early in the season. The village, however, is open year-round.

If your visit coincides with Halloween, there is only one place to be to celebrate it: Salem, scene of the historical witchcraft trials and home of the Witch Museum. This is Halloween at its most authentic, and each year the entire town hosts a wide range of events from zany to supernatural. A schedule of events is available from the Salem Chamber of Commerce, 32 Derby Square, Salem, Massachusetts 01970; (617) 744-

0004. If you want to get in the "spirit" of things, you can hear ghost stories in a darkened room at the Witch Museum for about $8, including refreshments. Also in Salem is the beautiful House of Seven Gables, setting for Nathaniel Hawthorne's classic tale.

Tucked in between the foliage are towns famous for their handcrafted items.

The whole Massachusetts countryside gets decked out for Halloween. Bright-red doors with straw wreaths, and on every porch stoop there lounges an engaging scarecrow or a menacing, black-hatted witch or a pile of bright-orange pumpkins. Many towns host costume parades and balls as well. At Normandy Farms Campground, you can join other campers and local townsfolk in a costume parade and dance, so don't forget to pack your costume.

Be sure to attend some of the fairs as you come across them in your travels. New England fairs are rural, wholesome fun and include everything from apple-pie baking to horse racing.

And there's so much more to look forward to in marvelous Massachusetts. Simply driving through the legendary Berkshires, Cape Cod, New Bedford and Rockport, for instance, is a multihued pleasure in autumn. No doubt you'll leave this New England state with as many reasons to return again as you had when you came for the first time.

Fall Hopping in the Finger Lakes

Waterfall watchers have a heyday in northern New York, especially during autumn's colorful reign

Patricia L. Barnes

Rushing water and moving ice created the landscape: deep, winding sluiceways, step-like sheets of shale and crystal-clear pools are everywhere. These are the falls of New York's Finger Lakes. Carved into rock that was deposited before the dinosaurs reigned, they are falls that make you realize the awesome impact the natural elements can have on a single area.

Take Robert Treman State Park. A series of 12 waterfalls line the three-mile gorge, where each view is better than the last. The upper gorge boasts a waterfall known as Lucifer Falls, where white, frothy water descends to a deep gorge below.

What makes Lucifer Falls and the other falls in the Finger Lakes even more amazing is how they were formed. This area of New York was

PHOTO: NEW YORK PARKS, RECREATION & HISTORIC PRESERVATION

PHOTO: PATRICIA L. BARNES

Facing page, *The many falls of Finger Lakes state parks are easily assessible to the RVer.* This page, *This angler tries to get a strike in the lower Taughannock Falls State Park.*

Above, ***Small scenic falls are everywhere in this region. Trails are slippery and should be executed with care. Guided tours are available.*** **Below,** ***Located at the upper gorge park at Robert Treman State Park, this old mill is over a century old.***

host to several glacial advances and retreats in the last few 100,000 years. The last ended around 10,000 years ago, and, as it retreated, it flooded the region with millions of gallons of melted glacial water.

As the water cascaded over steep valley walls, rugged gorges formed, cut into the soft shales that covered the region. Areas that were more resistant to the surging water gave way to waterfalls. Even today, the relentless water continuously carves deeper into the rock.

PHOTO: DAVID W. TUTTLE

For the traveler in search of the ultimate waterfall, the many falls in the Finger Lakes state parks are easily accessible and worth the trip. For example, Buttermilk Falls, Robert Treman and Taughannock Falls State Parks—all have falls within a half-hour drive of each other.

The falls are easy to visit because of the numerous park facilities and trail systems. According to the Finger Lake State Parks office, many of the trails and walkway steps were built by the Civilian Conservation Corps (CCC) and the Work Progress Administration (WPA) during the Great Depression of the early 1930s. The trails and walkways are made from sandstone and shale taken from various sections of the gorge. The rock was placed, stone by stone, along the gorge, often on perilously steep rock faces. One amazing view is found along the gorge trail at Robert Treman; an overlook will take you 400 feet above the upper gorge.

PHOTO: N.Y. PARKS, RECREATION & HIST. PRESERVATION

Do not be put off by the names that surround the Finger Lakes. They are mostly Indian names and carry a proud heritage. Dozens of Indian tribes lived near the falls area until around the late 1700s. After the Indians came a time of industrialization; the falls were used to power small mills and gun factories during the 1800s. Today, the mills are gone from the area, and the falls are being preserved for their natural beauty.

The best way to "falls hop" is to start from Spencer, New York, and take State Highway 96 north. This route will take you to the lower Robert H. Treman State Park, where you can hike the three-mile trail to the top of the gorge. Enfield Creek rushes through Robert H. Treman State Park, twisting and turning its way toward the lower park, splashing over small and large waterfalls. All along the trail are "fire and brimstone" names—for example, the 115-foot Lucifer Falls at the top of the park and Devil's Kitchen in between. A century-old mill, now a museum of antique milling machinery, is located at the upper gorge. Visitors will enjoy the view of a small waterfall from the mill's second-floor covered porch.

There are also camping facilities for RVs, comfort stations and cabins at the lower park; the upper park contains a camping area and parking. Altogether there are close to 70 campsites and 14 cabins at the park.

Buttermilk Falls State Park is next on State Highway 96, where smaller but nonetheless beautiful falls await you. The area is rich with history. The entrance of Buttermilk State Park on Highway 96 leads to the middle of Buttermilk Creek. A short walk along a road and trail lined with hardwoods reveals an amazing sight: the huge Scott's Dam, which holds back water in a scenic man-made pool. From 1875 to 1912, this impoundment supplied the city of Ithaca with water. Now it is used for water-runoff control at the park.

Park Road to the south leads to Treman Lake. This is the start of the winding Buttermilk Creek and there is a picnic area and comfort station. A scenic trail winds around Treman Lake, with several stops and shelters along the way.

Three and a half miles from Treman Lake is the lower Buttermilk Falls State Park. Buttermilk Falls has a popular spot to swim in a stream-fed gorge pool. Located on State Highway 13 as you drive through Ithaca, it is an area with plenty of parking for picnics and 60 campsites where RVs are more than welcome.

Following Highway 96 to Ithaca will soon take you to State Highway 89 and Taughannock (pronounced "Tah-can-ock") Falls State Park. The "Great Falls in the Woods" is said to be the highest straight-drop falls in the northeastern United States—over 215 feet of water plunging into a deep pool at the bottom of a steep cliff.

From March to October, you can view Taughannock Falls from the ground up or top down. The upper park has a trail to an overlook, a short walk from a parking lot. The lower park also has parking facilities, with the trail leading three-quarters of a mile to the bottom falls. Also located at the lower falls are 76 campsites. There is plenty of parking across the street, so RVers can enjoy the park's additional amenities where Taughannock Creek enters Cayuga Lake.

For those people who tend more toward city life, there are the numerous falls in Ithaca, home of Cornell University. There is a gorge that marks the north boundary of the campus along Fall Creek.

The area around Ithaca offers the falls seeker many options, all within a short drive of each other. For those who want to see more of the Finger Lakes and the falls, there is always Watkins Glen—only a Finger Lake away to the west on State Highway 79 from Ithaca—or Filmore Glen, south of Moravia on State Highway 38, just off the tip of Owasco Lake.

Most of the Finger Lakes parks are open for RV camping from late March to mid-October, but there are exceptions; the lower park at Robert H. Treman doesn't close until early December. For other activities, the Finger Lakes parks are open year-round but, for safety reasons, there are some restrictions. Many rim and gorge trails are closed for the winter because of ice, and heavy rains and snowmelt may postpone the reopening of trails in the spring.

For more information on the falls of the Finger Lakes, contact: Finger Lakes State Parks, Recreation and Historic Preservation Region, Box 283, T.D. #3, Trumansburg, New York 14886-0721; or State Parks, Albany, New York 12238.

Waterfall hopping can become one of your most enjoyable RV experiences. It seems to be a well-kept secret—so few know about the mysteries and natural beauty that surround the falls of the Finger Lakes. It is up to you to explore the area and choose its loveliest falls. You may have a hard time deciding.

THE SOUTH

Creole Nature Trail

Deep in the Cajun heartland of Louisiana, discover a world of tranquil beauty

Peter M. Lewis

If the thought of traveling through an area where egrets are as common as pigeons is appealing, then consider a trip along the Creole Nature Trail in Louisiana. The state boasts over 3,500 square miles of water surface, including 5,000 acres of certified marsh. It's estimated that nearly a third of all North American bird species are either permanent or winter residents of the area, including the largest populations of blue and snow geese in North America. The delta region of the state serves as the southern terminus of the famed Mississippi flyway and plays host to an estimated 5 million ducks every winter.

The nature trail extends roughly from Lake Charles in the west to New Iberia in the east and traverses the southernmost roads in the state. New Iberia, a city three hours from New Orleans, is, in my view, one of the most interesting towns in the Cajun heartland of Louisiana.

I started the trip at Sam Houston Jones State Park, located 12 miles north of Lake Charles, just off U.S. Highway 171 in the southwestern part of the state. The 1,068-acre park sits at the juncture of Houston River and Indian Bayou and provides the visitor with a good introduction to Louisiana bayou country. The term bayou comes from the Choctaw Indian word for creek, *bayuk*.

The park has all the amenities required by the most demanding RV traveler, including ample pull-through campsites for those who desire them, and hot showers. There is playground equipment for those with small children and enough space that people are not packed together. In fact, it is a rare park that affords as much peace and solitude as this one. It is close enough to all the area attractions that it can be utilized as a base camp or simply used as a stop on an extended journey.

I camped at the park that first night and awoke early the next morning to experience the sunrise over one of the lagoons. Making my way to the water's edge, I began to sense the feeling that would typify the entire

Louisiana hosts large numbers of common waterfowl, such as this coot, in addition to exotic birds.

PHOTOS: PETER M. LEWIS

Left, *The alligator population in Louisiana has been estimated at 500,000.* Center, *Camping at Sam Houston Jones State Park is a great way to get acquainted with bayou country.* Right, *Blue crabs bring thirty-eight cents a pound to local wholesalers, who sell them for around three dollars a dozen.*

trip: tranquility. Picture, if you will, a small, still lake with stands of bald cypress trees positioned randomly over the surface like chessmen on a board. There are no long, clear vistas; you cannot see more than a few hundred yards in any direction without your view being obstructed by cypress. The cypress are cloaked in a translucent mantle of gray Spanish moss, ephemeral in the early morning light. The shoreline is heavily wooded, the ground covered with fallen leaves. Off in the distance, a lone white heron stands in the shallows, waiting. There are no motorboats, water skiers or marinas. Were there a boat, it would be a pirogue, or a canoe. Only the occasional trumpeting of a white-fronted goose, off in the distance, breaks the silence.

In the solitude of the park lagoons, you become aware of an abundance of waterfowl; the ubiquitous mallards, to be sure, but also many that have you reaching for your field guides: canvasbacks, teal and pintails, ring-necked coots and wood ducks, Canada and white-fronted geese. Nutria and armadillo are also common sights, best seen at sunset.

When the spirit moves, it is time to set out, driving south on State Highway 27 past the village of Hackberry, named for the tree of the same name. The town and environs are known for blue crabs, and in the vicinity you will find people fishing for them from practically every bridge, levee and road pull-off that you pass. Some use nets, but most folks attach a chicken wing to a line or standard fishing rod and wait for a crab to fasten itself to the bait, then pull it in to be deposited in a pail until suppertime; nothing exotic, but eminently successful. "Keepers" must measure 5 inches across. If you have children, let them experience the thrill of a fishing experience that assures a high probability of success.

Not far past Hackberry lies one of the jewels of the trail, the Sabine National Wildlife Refuge. The reserve consists of 142,846 acres of both brackish and freshwater pools, some 1,000 acres in size. It was established in 1937, primarily as a wintering area for the snow geese and ducks migrating down the Mississippi and central flyways. It also serves as home for the American alligator, the red wolf and the peregrine falcon. Better than 250 species of birds have been observed here by refuge staff and other ornithologists.

PHOTOS: PETER M. LEWIS

A thick border of trees along a lagoon adds to the mystery at Sam Houston Jones State Park. The common egret, a member of the heron family, is a bayou local, except in winter when it migrates to South America.

If you are not familiar with wildlife refuges, it is important to understand that they are not like parks, in that they offer very little in the way of visitor amenities. There is no camping, usually little in the way of exhibits, no book stores and so forth. They are primarily intended to provide habitat where wildlife can exist free of human interference. Sabine, for example, essentially has two areas open to the public, a grit site and a one-mile walking trail. From October through mid-March, blue and snow geese can often be seen at the grit site early in the morning. Geese require grit to grind their food for digestion. The walking trail extends out into the marsh, often on raised platforms, and is one of the most inspiring one-mile jaunts anywhere, if you enjoy viewing wildlife. It will quickly render all but the most comprehensive bird guides useless, until you give up attempting to identify all the species and just marvel at the variety. There are roseate spoonbills, white and white-faced ibis, Louisiana and little blue herons and abundant alligators to whet your appetite. Unless you visit between November and February, you may see alligators.

The refuge headquarters is located just a few miles south of Hackberry, where you can get a map of the walking trail and directions to the grit site. The trail itself is four miles past the headquarters building, just off the highway, and is well marked.

Leaving the Sabine Refuge, the next stretch of trail affords no camping opportunities until you reach the New Iberia area. That is the next logical place to stay overnight, unless you return to Sam Houston Jones State Park. The latter is 94 miles from New Iberia by the most direct route, so that option is eminently viable. As of this writing, there is one public campground close to New Iberia that is open year-round. It is Lake Fausse State Park, located in St. Martinville. If you are headed east, you may wish to stop at Grand Isle State Park in Grand Isle on the Gulf Coast. It allows camping on the beach and is popular with RVers who enjoy that setting. However, it is a long two-hour drive from New Iberia.

Private campgrounds in the area include the Abbeville Camper-Trailer Park in Abbeville, Sher-Mac Incorporated in New Iberia and a KOA campground 23 miles away in Lafayette. Consult the current edition of the *1989 Trailer Life Campground & RV Services Directory* for complete details. A *Louisiana Campgrounds Directory* (private) and a *State Parks Guide* are available for the asking from the Department of Culture, Recreation and Tourism, P.O. Drawer 1111, Baton Rouge, Louisiana 70821; (504) 925-3830.

State Highway 27 ends several miles past the refuge at the town of Holly Beach, primarily a weekend retreat on the Gulf of Mexico. There it intersects State Highway 82, which parallels the Gulf Coast. Heading east, the first town of note will be Cameron. Not far from Cameron is the next major wildlife area accessible to the public, the Rockefeller Wildlife Refuge at Grand Chenier. Consisting of 84,000 acres, it is owned and operated by the Louisiana Department of Wildlife and Fisheries. The Rockefeller facility serves a serious research function, including an important fisheries nursery area for southwestern Louisiana. The facilities are open to the public daily, including an approximately four-mile road into the marsh where waterfowl, wading birds and alligators may be observed in their natural environments. If you have a boat, access is available to much of the refuge with an appropriate permit. It has been estimated that upward of 400,000 ducks winter in the refuge. Permits are available at the refuge headquarters in Grand Chenier.

Past the Rockefeller Refuge, Highway 82 continues to parallel the Gulf Coast, eventually terminating at the intersection with State Highway 14 at the town of Abbeville. Taking Highway 14 east to New Iberia, you reach the last of the stops on the trail, Avery Island, the home of Tabasco Sauce.

If you need a respite from all of that nature, New Iberia has much to offer in its own right. It lies in the heart of Acadiana, Cajun country. Of particular interest are The Shadows on the Teche and Mintmere Plantation, antebellum mansions, the Konriko Rice Mill (the oldest operating rice mill in America) and Jefferson Gardens, the former summer home of Joseph Jefferson, who in the late 1800s was reputedly the most famous actor in America. The gardens surrounding the home are truly spectacular.

Avery Island is a six-mile hop from downtown New Iberia and a fitting finish to the Creole Nature Trail. Avery Island is actually a salt dome, a plug of salt eight miles deep and six miles in circumference at the surface. It is one of six such formations in the New Iberia area. As an indication of scale, Mount Everest would fit easily inside the dome. Salt is mined through a shaft extending 530 feet into the earth.

Avery Island was the home of Edward Avery McIlhenny, founder of the company that manufactures Tabasco Sauce. When he wasn't presiding over the production of hot sauce, McIlhenny wrote books (*Autobiography of an Egret, Life History of the Alligator*), bred plants (camellias were a passion) and attempted single-handedly to save the egret from extinction. He also turned his home into an immense garden, the cultivated portions of which exceed 250 acres.

To a nature lover, probably the most interesting tale related to this remarkable man was his work on behalf of the egret. At mating time, egrets sport special plumage or aigrettes. In the latter part of the last century, plume hunters had almost decimated the egret population to meet the market demand for feathers used to adorn ladies' hats. Since the aigrettes were only worn during mating season, the killing of the birds was doubly tragic, not only causing the death of the parent but insuring the demise of any offspring as well.

The story goes that a British official who was visiting the McIlhenny home told a story of an Indian rajah who had constructed large cages of bamboo to house exotic birds brought to his kingdom to impress his queen. After the rajah's death, the cages fell into disrepair, rotted and were lost, but the birds remained, though there were no cages to restrain them. Inspired by the tale, McIlhenny took it upon himself to go into the swamps of Louisiana and capture seven young snowy egrets, for which he constructed a special cage on an artificial lake on the compound at Avery Island. He nurtured the birds to maturity, watched them raise their young and, at the start of the migratory season, destroyed the cage to let nature take its course and allow the birds to follow their instincts for their annual pilgrimage to South America. The following spring, the birds returned to Avery Island and began a colony that now contains 20,000 nests constructed during mating season each spring in the section of the property known as Bird City.

The gardens of Avery Island are beautiful in their own right, with thousands of azalea and camellia plants and untold others from around the world. With 250 acres to roam, visitors can take as short or long a tour as personal interest dictates. There is a road through the gardens, the beauty of which will satisfy the casual visitor, and a series of garden paths for those who wish to linger.

Apart from the formal attractions, the roads of the Creole Nature Trail usually parallel either the Gulf of Mexico or one of the many bayous of southern Louisiana. The bayous meander slowly through the countryside, past rusting, corrugated-metal boat houses and children fishing for bass, crappie or catfish. They're often clogged with water hyacinths and duckweed. The roads are rural, with nothing to invite commerce, and thus can be traveled at a leisurely pace. For RV wanderers, it is an area of charm, inspiration and tranquility.

NORTH AND CENTRAL

Superior Playground

Along the shoreline of Lake Superior lies some of the country's finest scenic and recreational land

Robert J. and Geraldine R. Smith

Indians harvest rice on lakes south of Bayfield Peninsula.

Looking for a land of clear streams, hundreds of lakes of all sizes, endless forest trails and a lakeshore that rivals the finest ocean coastline?

Want some place that is uncrowded and has plenty of campgrounds, where tourists are welcomed with open arms? Dreaming of a place where the fishing is fabulous, where anglers can land steelhead, chinook, trout, walleye, crappie, perch, bluegill, bass and more? How about bird watching, rock hounding, berry picking, canoeing, backpacking or just plain loafing around?

There is such a dream-come-true place: Lake Superior. You can throw a rock in any direction there and find something interesting to see or do wherever it lands. It is RVing country at its finest.

Lake Superior is the largest, deepest and highest of the Great Lakes, as well as the largest freshwater lake in the world. It is also a major waterway over which millions of tons of cargo pass each year. And, wonder of wonders, its sparkling blue waters are crystal clear and almost free of pollution.

Around its western terminus, at the twin ports of Duluth, Minnesota, and Superior, Wisconsin, an area known as the Head of the Lakes, lies

PHOTOS: ROBERT J. SMITH

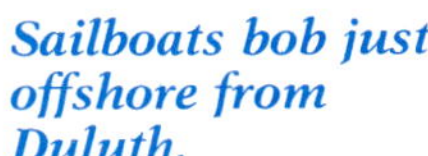

Sailboats bob just offshore from Duluth.

some of the finest scenic and recreational country in the United States. The cooling breezes off the great lake make the "dog days" of August unknown.

French explorers, who arrived in the area in the mid-1600s, started a progression of development that included fur trading, mining, lumbering, shipping and tourism. The latter is a mainstay of the economy with many once-casual visitors returning year after year.

Duluth, the area's largest city with a population of about 90,000, sprawls over the hillsides overlooking Lake Superior and the harbor. Its accommodations range from the rustic to sophisticated; the prices match the facilities.

There is much to see and do in this northern metropolis. The hills, which add to the city's charm, make RVing somewhat tricky; however, it is nothing to deter any but the most timid. Just keep your rig in low gear when towing or touring. If you prefer, the hills can be circumvented entirely.

Duluth's Skyline Drive, a scenic roadway 700 feet above lake level, features outstanding views of the city, harbor and surrounding countryside. The view from the top of Enger Tower is breathtaking.

The Aerial Lift Bridge, one of two such structures in the world, spans the ship canal at the entrance to Duluth's harbor. This unusual bridge rises 138 feet in less than a minute. The canal is narrow enough that spectators can talk with crew members as the great ships pass through. If the ship is a "saltie" (ocean-going ship), the replies can be in languages as diverse as the United Nations. No matter how unintelligible the words, sailors' smiles and waving arms are universal. The Canal Park Marine Museum at this location features interesting exhibits about the shipping industry and Great Lakes lore and legend.

Depot Square is a fascinating facet of the past. The old train depot, first opened in 1892, has been renovated and now serves as a museum and cultural center. The museum features rare items such as Minnesota's first locomotive (circa 1861), the first locomotive on the Northern Pacific Railroad, and *Engine No. 227*, a 566-ton, 128-foot-long behemoth—one of the world's largest steam locomotives. This museum is a train buff's delight.

PHOTO: ROBERT J. SMITH

Gooseberry Falls in on Lake Superior's North Shore Drive.

Campgrounds in the Head of the Lakes area are both plentiful and reasonably priced. Many are right by the water, which makes fishing and other water sports easy to enjoy for RV visitors.

PHOTO: ROBERT J. SMITH

Other prime attractions in Duluth are the Zoological Gardens, the Viking boat in Leif Ericson Park and Glensheen Mansion on the North Shore of Lake Superior.

The North Shore Drive along Lake Superior qualifies as one of this nation's great scenic drives. Breathtaking vistas open around each bend as the highway skirts the lakeshore. Many parks and picnic areas allow one to pull the rig over and soak up the scenery. Rock hounds can find the famous Lake Superior agates along many of the rocky beaches.

The tiny village of Knife River, a sport and commercial fishing center, calls itself the "smoked fish capital of the North Shore." It may or may not be, but the smoked fish sold there is delicious.

At Two Harbors' Paul Van Hoven Park you can watch giant ore carriers being maneuvered in and out of the port, and get a look at the *Edna G.*, the last hand-fired, coal-burning, steam-powered tug on the Great Lakes. This lovely craft, built in 1896, is still in operating condition. She is also on the National Register of Historic Sites.

If scuba diving is your thing, the wreck of the *Samuel P. Ely* lies in 25 to 30 feet of water at the breakwall in Agate Bay. This three-masted schooner was built in 1869 and sank on what was to be her last voyage. This is a popular dive and, although her masts are gone, the ship sits upright on the bottom as if underway. Inquire locally about diving. A beautiful municipally owned campground is located on the north shore of Two Harbors. It is just one of the many beautiful campgrounds in the area; check the *Trailer Life 1989 Campground & RV Services Directory* for others.

Gooseberry Falls State Park is a showcase for Lake Superior's rocky shoreline. It also features five tumbling waterfalls, the best of which can be viewed at the U.S. Highway 61 bridge, where the water tumbles over the 30-foot Upper Falls, then onto the two-tiered Lower Falls, plunging 60 feet into a pool. Daily or annual permits are required for the use of Minnesota's state parks. Overnight camping fees are also charged where applicable.

The north shore's most photographed subject is the classic Split Rock Lighthouse at Split Rock State Park. The lighthouse crowns a sheer cliff like a jewel in a natural setting. Its beacon, 168 feet above the mean water level, could be seen from 72 miles away. Modern navigational aids have made the lighthouse obsolete, but its future is assured as a state park.

Superior, the smaller of the Head of the Lakes cities, is reached from Duluth via a high bridge, which spans the harbor. The Superior entry to the harbor is at the tip of Wisconsin Point, an excellent place to picnic and watch the great ships. The Superior side of the port is home to the *S.S. Meteor.* Built in 1896, it is the sole survivor of a whaleback fleet that once numbered 43. She is now listed on the National Register of Historic Sites and is open for tours.

Superior's Fairlawn Historical Museum is housed in a 42-room mansion. The house, built for mining baron Martin Pattison, has been restored to original condition. It is a beautiful example of nineteenth-century Queen Anne architecture. It features carved panels of oak, cherry and maple as well as fireplaces trimmed in marble, onyx, gold and silver.

The drive along the south shore of Lake Superior around the Bayfield Peninsula, labeled the "Top o' Wisconsin," is one of the finest drives in the area. Although the lakeshore can be rugged, the countryside is mellower than that found north of the lake. Clearings in the forest often flash the smiles of a million daisies, and other wildflowers create a kaleidoscope of color that is not soon forgotten.

Nearly half of Bayfield County is publicly owned land, a situation that guarantees superb recreational opportunities. There are more than 1,000 sites for campers, and the welcome sign is always out.

Highlight of the Bayfield Peninsula is the beautiful Apostle Islands National Lakeshore, which consists of 12 miles of lakeshore and an archipelago of 22 islands. The archipelago's magnificent scenery is fashioned from sheer cliffs, sea waves, sandy coves and driftwood-littered beaches that are a delight to beachcombers. Island sizes range from tiny to the immense; 14,000-acre Madeline Island, the queen of the group, can be reached via a 15-minute ferry ride from Bayfield.

In bygone days the town of Bayfield was a popular destination point to which steamship companies and railroads brought thousands of excursionists. Those days are gone, but many modern RVers, once they discover the charm of the area, return every summer.

In season, strawberries are plentiful and delicious. The Bayfield berry holds a special niche in the hearts of gourmets. There is rarely a surplus, as local eaters seldom leave many for export.

The area around Chequamegon Bay, with its lush summer growth and abundant game supply, was long a bone of contention between the Sioux and Chippewa Indians. After a series of battles, the Sioux were defeated and drifted westward into Minnesota and onto the western prairies, where they clashed with the encroaching white settlers and soldiers. It is on the "shores of Gitchee Gumee, of the shining Big Sea Water" (thank you, Longfellow) that some of the best of the Head of the Lakes is awaiting discovery, truly the place where "summer comes to vacation."

Hoosier Heartland

Whether wandering Indiana's rural roads or city streets, RVers will thrill to basketball fever and racing mania

Martin Hintz

PHOTO: WILBUR MONTGOMERY

Medals rewarded 1987 Pan American Games' winners.

If America had to choose an official heartland, Indiana should win hands down. Images abound: county fairs, corn on the cob, the Wabash River, the Indy 500 auto race. The state is the quintessence of down-home America with its spacious summer-shaded porches, freshly made lemonade, driveway basketball games and red barns.

It's also a great RVing state, offering a lot more than simple interstate whizzing across the northern flatlands that link Illinois and Ohio. The state's tourism motto is "Wander Indiana," and there's hardly a better way of doing so than by driving its less-traveled highways and byways.

The name *Indiana* was coined in 1800 when the U.S. Congress pulled part or all of what would be five Midwestern states out of the old Northwest Territory. This hunk of wilderness rimming the Great Lakes—owned in succession by the French and British—consisted primarily of Indiana, Illinois, Michigan, Wisconsin and Minnesota. In 1812, after land trades made in smoke-filled cloakrooms, geopolitical boundaries were finally established for Indiana.

Indiana—meaning the "Land of the Indians"—was made a state in 1816. The state motto, "Crossroads of America," was adopted in 1937, commemorating generations of pioneers, traders, settlers and soldiers of fortune who meandered through the region.

Today's RV traveler can take in Indiana's burgeoning urban scene or wander the backroads to discover a dozen rural secrets. They aren't hard to find because the state is only 175 miles wide and 275 miles long.

PHOTO: BILL THOMAS

Beck's Mill in Salem is a picturesque stop for RVers interested in seeing the state's historical sights.

Pokagon State Park in Angola is one of many offering shaded sites.

PHOTO: MARTIN HINTZ

Northern Indiana, around Lafayette (home of football giant Purdue University), is especially great during the months of pigskin mania.

If cheerleading and hoopla aren't on the agenda, Fort Ouiatenon should be. The historical park on South River Road, four miles southwest of West Lafayette, is best visited in October when hundreds of voyageurs and Revolutionary War re-enactment groups from the North West Territory Alliance converge on the stockade for the Feast of the Hunter's Moon. The alliance, an association of more than 30 authentically eighteenth-century-garbed regiments, insures that there will be plenty of marching, black-powder musketry and fife-and-drum music. Indian dancing and blanket trading bring to mind the early frontier days. When the voyageurs swing down the Wabash River, singing their boisterous canoeing songs, a visitor can easily imagine it's 250 years ago.

The original trading outpost was built by the French in 1717. It was subsequently occupied by British troops and burned after the Revolutionary War under George Washington's orders. A replica blockhouse was reconstructed in 1930.

Admission to the feast at the time of this writing was $5 at the gate or $4 in advance per adult; youngsters 4 to 12, $2 at the gate or $1 in advance. For more details, contact the fort at 909 South Street, Lafayette, Indiana 47901; (317) 742-8411. Parking is available in nearby fields, which might pose a problem for heavier motorhomes and trailers if there's been a recent rain. Don't let that slow you down, however. Sometimes friendly neighbors allow parking in their driveways, most of which are spacious enough for all sizes of vehicles.

The Tippecanoe Battlefield State Memorial near the town of Battle Ground is another excellent stop, seven miles north of Lafayette. Only three miles east of Interstate 65 on State Highway 43, it's easily reached. Self-guided walking tours take in the once bloody ground where General William Henry Harrison defeated the Shawnees in their last desperate attempt to keep Yankee settlers out of tribal lands. The battle on November 7, 1811, ended Indian control over the region. Seeing the marked graves of the soldiers is sobering, but the spirits of the Indians are felt just as strongly in the early dusk, especially near Prophet's Rock, where the Indians mobilized for the attack.

Don't forget the nearby Tippecanoe Museum, open from 10 A.M. to 5 P.M., which presents an honest view of both sides of the battle. An

PHOTO: IMS BY STEVE SNODDY

PHOTO: MARTIN HINTZ

PHOTO: WILBUR MONTGOMERY

Left, Swimmers, such as this diver, gained international recognition during the 10th Pan American Games held in Indianapolis in August of 1987.* Top, *The Indianapolis 500 draws drivers and spectators from around the world every May.* Bottom, *Fishermen flock to Brown County's lakes and rivers.

85-foot-tall monument marks where Harrison's soldiers bivouacked. Plenty of surface parking available at the Tippecanoe site; I've never experienced any trouble driving in or out of the lots.

In another woodsy Indiana locale, however, even my Cub Scout training wasn't much help. I once got lost driving around sprawling Brown County State Park near Nashville, west of Bloomington in southern Indiana. The park is the largest in the state, covering some 15,428 acres of hills and valleys with horizon-to-horizon trees. And if that's not enough fresh lumber to observe, the 155,000-acre Hoosier National Forest is just next door. I must have taken a wrong turn or something during our day of hiking and picnicking because I couldn't get oriented properly on some of the more remote unmarked trails. We must have covered every backroad wide enough for our vehicle as we sought an exit from the bush. Delightful as the scenery was, enthusiasm was slim as night fell over the countryside. Somehow, we finally popped out of the wilderness just west of Gnawbone (love that name!).

By the way, Brown County's Nashville is quite an artists' colony. The village streets are lined with galleries and trendy studios where you can pick up fine art objects as well as country crafts. Prices range all over the place, of course. A don't-miss spot is the Brown County Art Guild on South Van Buren Street, which usually features Indiana artists.

On busy summer and autumn weekends, parking is a pain. Yet we always turn the problem into a plus by parking out of the crowded downtown area. Then, we can stroll through the village and visit backstreet shops that offer goods at lower prices than the more touristy places on the main thoroughfares.

While in southern Indiana, don't pass up an opportunity to drive to historic New Harmony, founded by Father George Rapp's Harmony Society in 1814. Hailed as the "Wonder of the Wilderness," the entire community was sold to Welsh industrialist Robert Owen a few years later. Owen, a social reformer as well as a manufacturer, had high hopes for the place, which became an intellectual and artistic center of the early Midwest. The community disintegrated after a decade of bickering and had disbanded by 1824.

Walking tours start at the Visitors Center on Church and Brewery streets. There are many art galleries, so don't forget your billfold or purse.

The village, in the far southwest section of Indiana on State Highway 66, is not far from the Illinois border. Burdette Park at nearby Evansville has 24 campsites available from April 1 to November 15, and Manager Mark Tuley can provide information on other recreational opportunities in the vicinity. Contact him at Burdette Park, Box 7081, Evansville, Indiana 47712; (812) 424-9535).

Indiana is one of several states that can claim "Abe Lincoln slept here." The Lincoln Boyhood Home National Memorial is on a tiny farm near Lincoln City in Spencer County. Costumed interpreters work at the site, tending crops similar to those grown by the Lincolns, who lived here from 1816 to 1830. This was a bittersweet place for young Lincoln. His mother, Nancy Hanks, is buried in a wooded grove not far from a log cabin built along the lines of Honest Abe's original house. The site is off State Highway 162 about two miles east of Gentryville and four miles south of Dale. One of the slickest ways to get there is to take U.S. Highway 231 south out of Dale to Gentryville. Signs mark the route.

About seven miles east of Gentryville, on Highway 162, is the town of Santa Claus. For the seasonal-minded shopper, every gift store in town sells Christmas ornaments.

Among the closest campgrounds to Indianapolis, the Circle City, is the 107-site, full-service Kamper Korner at 1951 West Edgewood Avenue; (317) 788-1488. The Fairland Recreation Park has 48 landscaped sites about 20 miles southeast of Indianapolis on Interstate 74. For information, call (317) 835-4617.

For additional campground information, see the *Hoosier Campground and RV Services Directory,* a comprehensive, complimentary booklet prepared by the Recreation Vehicle Indiana Council. To secure a copy, contact the council at 3210 Rand Road, Indianapolis, Indiana 46241; (317) 247-6258 or (800) 238-RVIC. Also helpful is the Tourism Development Division of the Indiana Department of Commerce, One North Capitol, Suite 700, Indianapolis, Indiana 46204-2288; (800) 2-WANDER.

There is a shuttle-bus system for motorists who prefer to park outside the congested area. Riders can park at any number of designated park-'n'-ride sites and hop aboard a metro bus. For more information, contact the Indianapolis Convention and Visitors Bureau, 100 S. Capital Avenue, Indianapolis, Indiana 46225; (317) 639-4282.

Indianapolis has parleyed itself into becoming the amateur sports capital of the United States. The city has staked its financial rebirth on encouraging amateur athletic organizations to homestead there. Indianapolis hosted the 1987 Pan Am games because of the $140-million investment in sports facilities around the area, ranging from the 70,000-seat Hoosier Dome to the Major Taylor Velodrome (named after Marshall "Major" Taylor, the first professional black athlete in the United States and winner of the National Cycling Championship in 1897).

The building boom included the Indiana University Natatorium, the university's track-and-field stadium, the Indianapolis Sports Center with its 24 clay and asphalt tennis courts and Market Square Arena, home of the Indiana Pacers pro basketball team.

The city still touts its rough-tough Indy 500 auto-race classic, and you can take a spin around the world-famous track in a minibus (except during the Memorial Day race). But you don't need to know how Indianapolis put itself back on the map to enjoy what it has to offer.

Most of the downtown is in fairly spiffy shape, with roadways open even for the largest motorhomes or trailers. There are ample municipal and private lots scattered throughout the area, so simply park and walk. This is a convenient town in which to get around. Be careful, however, about parking on the campus of the Indiana University–Purdue University at Indianapolis. Although there are 12,000 parking sites at the school, permits are required for most of them.

Construction may still obstruct some traffic in the vicinity of the White River State Park, being built near downtown to the tune of $150 million. A zoo, the first phase of the park, is scheduled for opening in 1988. Next on tap will be an amusement park, botanical gardens and a performing arts center.

You can spend days at the Children's Museum of Indianapolis, where the motto is "Please touch." In the event of rain, it's the best place in the world to keep the kids occupied. One of the best displays is the Passport to the World exhibit, where visitors can try on clothes from other nations. Youngsters delight in sticking their arms into a special projection box to see how they'd look covered with tattoos. The building is situated on five acres in the central city, at the corner of 30th and North Meridian streets, only a five-minute drive from Monument Circle. Admission is free, and there's plenty of parking space for RVs.

Union Station, a delightful warren of shops and eateries located in the city's fabled old train station, is located across from Pan Am Plaza and its two Olympic-quality ice-skating rinks. Developers Robert and Sandra Borns, who assembled the money for the multimillion-dollar station refurbishment, are confirmed RVers who spend their vacations driving around the country. In 1982, they seized on the chance to save the faded facility from the wrecker's ball and turned the building into a browser's paradise. Life-size statues of old-time travelers and train crews dot the station, causing more than one visitor to stop short and stare. Wisely, the artist kept his figures an off-white color. I can imagine the confusion if they looked too real.

For a change of pace from RVing, you might want to spend a night in a room in the Holiday Inn, built right into Union Station. Some of the fancier suites are in old train cars, each themed after an era when train travel was de rigueur.

I've never had any mechanical difficulty in the Hoosier State, but it was good to know that Indiana, which calls itself the RV capital of the nation, is also home to manufacturers of everything from fifth-wheel trailers to Class A motorhomes. Many sales outlets offer excellent servicing in emergency cases as well. Since most outlets can handle problems ranging from faulty wheel bearings to refrigeration, you can wander Indiana without a worry.

OK, let's see. I'm set to visit the Hoosier Heartland; now which county fair is held that week?

THE WEST

Spectacular waterfalls cascade along Sunsight Pass.

PHOTOS: FRED BURRIS

Stepping High

Glacier National Park attracts hikers with dozens of ice fields and mountain-high trails

Fred and Dora Burris

The majestic, primitive beauty of Glacier National Park cannot be exaggerated with too many adjectives—our visit to this western Montana treasure proved this. Standing at Grinnell Overlook, we looked down on incredible Grinnell Glacier for the first time. This 4,000-year-old, mile-long ice cube lay stretched below us, ignoring time and forming the final toehold of a V-shaped glacier cirque, a natural amphitheater. From our lofty perch in this part of the Rocky Mountains, we watched miniature-looking people walk along the edge of the frozen flow—just one of 60 glaciers in the park. Surrounded by a vast combination of ice, mountain and meadow, we were inspired to take in all the park's beauty and recreation opportunities—abundant though they are.

Having left our RV at the parking lot near Logan Pass Visitors Center, we had just hiked the Highline Trail. The path wends its way high above the glacier-carved basins, undulates along the Garden Wall, and skirts the Continental Divide. For the most part, it is open terrain with wildflowers blooming at their august peak. Cow parsnip rising higher than our heads tend to choke out the trail. The spur to Grinnell Overlook is one kilometer. We retrace this portion of the rocky indentation. Indian paintbrush in brilliant orange and yellow puffs called sulphur flowers bobbing in the breeze are dwarf varieties of their counterparts, which are abundant at lower elevations. It is nature's rock garden.

Wild mountain goats are frequently seen on Gunsight Pass.

A 2.1-mile hike to St. Mary's Falls presents incomparable mountain scenery and can be made on your own or with a naturalist guide.

We can see Granite Park Chalet in the distance. Our canteens are dry. We begin to savor the thought of the cold drink we'll have when we get there. Built out of available native stone on a projection of rock, Granite Park Chalet commands the best view around. Mountain peaks surround it. Three major trails converge near it. Numerous hikers stop here for a pleasant exchange of trail information, a hearty meal or, if they have reservations, a night's rest. (All park chalets require advance reservations, and peak summer accommodations are usually filled by March.)

The evening meal at the chalet is a time for getting acquainted. Introductions are made all around, revealing occupations such as doctor, clergyman, teacher, student and so on. Wherever people are from, all agree, "We'll be back!"

Before the sun made its retreat behind Heaven's Peak, Fred spotted a grizzly bear in nearby Bear Valley. A spotting scope was set up on a picnic table. Three grizzlies were seen feeding in the alpine meadows.

PHOTO: FRED BURRIS

You might think you would have to travel to the Swiss or Austrian Alps to experience staying in a rustic mountain chalet, but two are located right in Glacier National Park. Both are in unsurpassable settings, accessible by foot or horseback. In addition to Granite Park, there is Sperry Chalet, six miles from glacier-fed McDonald Lake, where you can hire horses for a day trip. The bridle path here winds its way through a cedar forest and up all the way, making the horseback ride up and hiking back pleasant trips.

If you are a vigorous hiker, you may choose to hike from the St. Mary's side of Glacier, traversing over Gunsight Pass. It is a 14-mile route that offers a variety of topography: a pine forest, waterfalls and glimpses of Jackson Glacier. Crossing a swinging bridge near the outlet of Gunsight Lake, the trail gradually climbs to the pass. As you take a breather here, a visual feast is spread out before you. The deep fuchsia of fireweed in its multiblossomed stems is a wave of color against the Persian blue of the deep-set lake, fed by a myriad of waterfalls. We counted nine from one viewpoint.

Wending your way past snowbanks that produce one or more waterfalls, you will finally gain the summit. Straddling the Continental Divide—Gunsight Lake on one side and Lake Ellen Wilson on the other—is a stone cabin. Mountain goats amble about, peaks rise skyward, unmelted snow and ice cling to the knife-edged cliffs. It is like being in a scene from *Heidi*. One almost expects to see Grandfather stepping out of the cabin. In reality, it is a shelter for travelers, a refuge from wind or sudden storms.

Dropping down to the valley, we met several hikers. They ranged in age from teenagers to retirees. Most had spent the night at Sperry Chalet and were on their way out.

When planning a hiking trip in Glacier, there are two tips that will make it easier for you to enjoy what awaits you on Glacier's trails.

PHOTO: ROBERT J. SMITH

Glacier National Park offers breathtaking sights when driving the Going-to-the-Sun Road.

The park's well-maintained Going-to-the-Sun Road delights RV travelers with panoramic vistas at every turn, including this alpine scene at Logan Pass.

Wearing comfortable clothes is a must, from shoes or hiking boots to jackets and rain gear. Another handy item is a daypack for carrying an extra jacket, rain gear, lunch and camera accessories.

Plan to include in your itinerary one or two short hikes after arriving in Glacier, to acclimate yourself to the mountain environment. There are several you can take on your own or with a ranger naturalist, such as one to St. Mary's Falls, a 2.1-mile hike from Sun Point, around Swift Current Lake; a 1.6-mile walk from the Many Glacier Hotel or Hidden Lake Overlook; or a 1.5-mile climb from Logan Pass Visitors Center.

PHOTO: ROBERT J. SMITH

At present, there is no public bus or commuter service in Glacier, so towing a compact car can be very advantageous. Having a vehicle to leave at a destination point, you can go in one way and return another, thus expanding your experience.

Top, *Off the Highline Trail, Grinnell Overlook gives visitors a bird's-eye view of Grinnell Glacier.* Bottom, *If you're lucky and observant, you may spot a ptarmigan on one of the park's many trails.*

For instance when we outlined our trip to Sperry Chalet via Gunsight Pass, we took our car to the McDonald Lake concession area near the trail head and drove our RV to the Gunsight Trail head on the St. Mary's side of Glacier, where we began. This enabled us to do the hardest and longest stint before reaching Sperry Chalet. By using our towed vehicle, there was no backtracking, providing us with twice as much scenic beauty. Of course Glacier National Park offers many such hiking opportunities.

There is one key regulation to be aware of when drafting your schedule: Vehicles exceeding 30 feet aren't allowed to drive the entire Going-to-the-Sun Road. If your RV combination exceeds this ordinance, you will want to study the alternatives. Checking with the visitors center at the entrance when you arrive will help. Write in advance for trail maps and request one for camping in the backcountry. For such information, contact: Superintendent, Glacier National Park, West Glacier, Montana 59936; (406) 888-5441.

PHOTOS: FRED BURRIS

Wherever you go with your RV in Glacier, you're sure to enjoy the view. Stepping high in Glacier, you'll truly experience the vast backcountry, adding a dimension to your RV vacation that will last forever.

Colter Country

Yellowstone and Grand Teton national parks have been mesmerizing generations with their haunting, majestic beauty

Glenn and Maxine Bamburg

In the late autumn of 1808, mountain man John Colter grew careless in Wyoming country and, as a consequence, was captured by a roving band of Blackfoot Indians. A sporting chance for his life was offered if he could outrun twenty of the swiftest braves. The added handicap of being stripped of his clothing and footwear slowed Colter to some degree, but sheer desperation aided his successful flight.

PHOTO: GLENN BAMBURG

Old Faithful performs religiously for today's travelers.

Reaching the waters of a rushing river, the toughened Virginian plunged in and hid for hours beneath a collection of debris until the searching warriors gave up, thinking he had drowned in the icy stream. Eighteen months later, Colter once again escaped certain death at the hands of the Blackfeet.

It proved to be Colter's final ordeal in this wild and beautiful land. Swearing he had seen enough, the man destined to become a legend journeyed to Missouri, where he died in poverty four years later.

Colter is credited today as the first white man to discover and explore the magnificent areas that we know as Grand Teton and Yellowstone national parks. To fellow trappers, however, his wondrous tales of steaming geysers and bubbling cauldrons of mud were believed to be the fantasy of an overactive imagination, and his reported discoveries were mocked for many years as "Colter's Hell."

PHOTO: GLENN BAMBURG

Trail riders meander through Lupine Meadows at the base of the Tetons.

Sulphuric steam rises from a pool in the Fountain Paint Pot Nature Trail area.

Grand Teton National Park has commemorated the exploits of this mountain man by naming its largest visitor complex after him: Colter Bay. Here and in the rest of the 500-square-mile park, a wide variety of recreational activities can be enjoyed by RVers beneath the shadows of craggy, cloud-high peaks.

Open from late June to late August, the five main campgrounds provide a more convenient access for exploring the Tetons than Colter had in the early 1800s. A total of 950 campsites are available on a first-come, first-served basis.

PHOTOS: GLENN BAMBURG

The Snake River, which courses through the park, is a popular source of recreation for outdoor enthusiasts. Several concessionaires within the park boundaries offer scenic boat trips down the historic waterway that has been known by many names. During the span of more than a century and a half, the Snake River, as it is now known, has also been referred to as the Lewis, Shoshone, Mad, Saptin, Nez Perce and Sagebrush, among other names. Whether its final name was chosen because of the serpentine course it travels or for the Indians who lived along its banks remains a mystery.

Float excursions down the Snake River range from two hours to full-day trips with breakfast, lunch and dinner cookouts available. The general price ranges from $12.50 to $20, with an additional cost for meals. Sightings of moose, elk, deer, geese and countless other native creatures add excitement and an unforgettable thrill to the adventure.

Onshore activities include the challenge of fly-fishing. Park waters are among the last wild refuges of the cutthroat trout. Identified by bright-red slash marks under the throat and small black spots on the yellow-bronze body, the Snake River cutthroat is found only in the river's watershed and is a spirited game fish when hooked. Trout season in rivers and streams runs from April 1 through October 31 and requires a Wyoming state fishing license.

The sparkling waters of Jenny Lake (elevation 6,779 feet) and those of Leigh Lake (elevation 6,878 feet) are connected by a narrow mile-long body of water appropriately called String Lake. The two lakes are also joined in romantic tragedy, being named for an 1880s' trapper, Richard Leigh, and his Shoshone wife, Jenny.

Living in a one-room cabin with their six children, the entire family fell ill with smallpox. Leigh watched helplessly as his wife and children died one by one, until he alone survived in the snowbound cabin.

One of the best ways to enjoy the peaceful reflections of these lakes is by canoe. Rental canoes are available in the park for those who don't bring their own. A permit is required for all boats used here.

The Exum School of Mountaineering is located at the south end of Jenny Lake. Experts give on-the-spot training in the proper procedure for all phases of mountain climbing. Even the novice climber learns enough during the first day of instruction to make a practice climb under the watchful eyes of a qualified staff member.

For those more practiced in the art of mountaineering, the up-reaching spires of the Tetons present some of North America's most inspiring

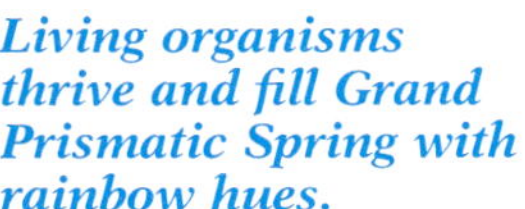

Living organisms thrive and fill Grand Prismatic Spring with rainbow hues.

challenges. They demand both knowledge and skill gained from years of experience, and a thorough briefing from park rangers is advisable. Registration is required for all climbers.

Exum offers classes for intermediate and advanced climbers, as well as beginners. Rental equipment is available to students, and all techniques of the sport are taught during intensive training sessions.

Hiking is another excellent way to witness the grandeur of the Tetons. More than 200 miles of well-maintained hiking trails are provided. They range from short, easy nature walks to strenuous hikes and overnight treks into the backcountry.

The hiker often returns to camp with an entirely different outlook on the Teton area. For those who search, the forest shares her natural secrets, while the mountains and valleys unfold their intriguing beauty.

To the north of Jenny and Leigh lakes, Jackson Lake forms the largest mirror to reflect the towering peaks of the Tetons. Covering almost 26,000 acres, the lake is more than 16 miles long, with a total shoreline of 81 miles. One can only imagine the reaction of John Colter as he stood on the banks and admired the awesome spectacle of the mountains on the west shore, jutting some 7,000 feet above the lake's shining surface.

PHOTO: GLENN BAMBURG

Midway Geyser Basin warms the waters of the Firehole River.

Early Indians, trappers and hunters must have viewed the Teton region from horseback, and today's visitor can enjoy the scenery from the same perspective. Saddle horses are available for trail rides from Jackson Lake Lodge, Jenny Lake, Jenny Lake Lodge and Colter Bay.

One-, two- and three-hour rides provide easy access across meadows overflowing with colorful lupine, and around Jenny Lake to Hidden Falls. Longer trail rides allow visitors to venture out for a full day to secluded Lake Solitaire. For those who are interested, overnight pack trips take riders into higher and more isolated areas.

Breakfast trail rides whet the appetite as bacon sizzles over an open campfire. An evening on-the-trail steak fry is enhanced by an outstanding survey of starry skies above the shadowed peaks.

Additional recreation in Grand Teton includes interpretive programs conducted by rangers. Movies, slides, shows, museums and historical displays at the visitors center offer a wealth of park information. Ranger-led nature hikes, investigative wildflower excursions and canoe trips are regularly scheduled services. Campfire programs are held each evening, with a wide range of topics which are posted on the visitors center bulletin boards.

The journey from Grand Teton National Park north along the John D. Rockefeller Parkway to the world's largest collection of steaming geysers and bubbling mud pots is much easier for today's RVers to travel than it was for Colter. However, the spellbinding effect of Yellowstone's natural phenomena remains the same.

The fantastically eerie world of "hidden fires, smoking pits and gloomy terrors," as described by Colter, was shunned by natives, who thought it haunted by evil spirits. Early French trappers bestowed the name *Roche Jaune,* which translates to "Yellow Rock."

It is impossible to list or describe the countless sights of thermal phenomena, vast canyons, teeming wildlife, forested slopes and tumbling rivers found in Yellowstone's 2 million acres.

These features were not publicly recognized until 1870, when a curious party including a bank president, two merchants, a lawyer, an assessor and a revenue collector explored the region. Two years later, President Ulysses S. Grant established our first national park to preserve nature in the same unaltered state as Colter first viewed them.

The immensity of Yellowstone and its offerings presents today's visitor with the choice of staying long enough to see it all or merely squeezing in what time permits. Each of the five entrances joins Grand Loop Road, which winds around about 140 miles, passing most of the major attractions. Signs beside the roadway direct motorists to tune their radios to a specific frequency on which information is given about campsites, fees, scenic walks, etc.

More than 200 active geysers and 3,000 hot springs are within the boundaries of the dying volcanic area. Boardwalks provide a safe access for walking through the basins, where nature's showy displays hold your bewildered attention.

Predicted times of geyser eruptions are posted at the Old Faithful

Visitors Center. A stroll around the Upper Geyser Basin reveals numerous other geysers spouting steam and sprays of heated water. Many small pools are wondrous spectacles, with their surrounding borders colored with rainbow hues of algae growing in the warm water.

Some geysers don't abide by a timetable. Steamboat, in the Norris Geyser Basin, shoots water 300 to 350 feet into the air, but only erupts once a year—if that often. Dark Cavern and Constant, on the other hand, erupt several times an hour, reaching 10 to 40 feet high.

Today's geological expertise provides us with an explanation concerning the creation of geysers, a service unavailable in Colter's day. We know now that a geyser is a type of hot springs heated by hot rocks below the earth's surface. Steam bubbles upward, expanding as it nears the top of the water column, until the bubbles become too large and numerous to pass through tight spots. At a certain point, the bubbles actually lift the water, forcing it from the vent in a superheated shower of nature.

Hot springs are closely related to geysers, except that their underground channel systems permit circulation of the heated waters. In the Mammoth Hot Springs area, travertine terraces have been formed through the years by limestone deposits carried to the surface by the hot water. An astounding 500 gallons of water flow from Mammoth Hot Springs *each minute* with an estimated two tons of limestone brought to the surface daily.

The magnificent Grand Canyon of the Yellowstone is one of nature's greatest sculpturing projects. The Yellowstone River roars through 24 miles of golden-hued cliffs, carving the chasm more than 1,500 feet deep in some areas.

Two waterfalls plunge in thunderous glory. The lower one is twice the height of Niagara Falls. Uncle Tom's Trail descends about halfway down into the canyon (700 steps), ending a few yards in front of the Lower Falls for the convenience of nature lovers and photographers.

Yellowstone National Park has become synonymous with wildlife. Although the abundance may not be quite the same as in Colter's day, the wide variety is still present. Many of the 60 species of larger mammals such as deer, moose, elk and buffalo can be seen from the Grand Loop. Smaller animals, including coyotes, lynx, ground squirrels and marmots, also venture near the roadways. Bird watchers may spy a large portion of the more than 200 species. Bald eagles, trumpeter swans and osprey are among the feathered inhabitants of the forests and lakes of Yellowstone.

Black bears, once seen along the park roads, tend to roam the backcountry today, feeding on its natural bounty. The ferocious grizzly also calls Yellowstone home, although he, too, usually prefers the remote wilderness areas. Backpackers and hikers are cautioned to make noise as they walk in order to avoid startling a resident bear, and to be constantly aware that bears may be present anywhere in the park.

Since the exploration of John Colter, the seasons of more than 150 years have rolled past the Tetons and the fiery region known as Colter's Hell. Countless multitudes have viewed the wondrous sites since that time, and each one who visits comes away a little richer for having seen the essence of this American wilderness at its best!

Stone Rainbows

Dominated by haunting and spectacular sandstone formations, southeastern Utah remains a land of Western legends

Glenn and Maxine Bamburg

The steady labor of nature's molding forces in southeastern Utah is never completed. Time is measured in this red-rock region by the millions of years required to form the magnificent rainbow arches, spires and deep canyons dotting the landscape.

Selecting the historic town of Moab as our focal point for exploring the area, we were soon informed by her friendly citizens about the wide array of attractions to be enjoyed in this vast and tireless land.

Located on the Colorado River, Moab is a city rich in history. It sits on the ruins of an ancient Pueblo Indian village dating back to the eleventh and thirteenth centuries. The Spanish Trail crossed the river here in the 1830s and 1840s, forded by adventuresome men carrying trade goods between New Mexico and California.

In 1855, Mormon missionaries attempted to settle the area, establishing the Elk Mountain Mission. The mission was abandoned within three months, however, when Ute Indians attacked and killed three of the missionaries, and a permanent settlement was not realized until the late 1870s.

Landscape Arch is the longest known natural arch in the world.

PHOTOS: GLENN BAMBURG

Early Moab had a Wild West reputation. A prospector visiting Moab in 1891 reported that it was known as

Delicate Arch is one of the spectacular sights offered by Arches National Park's many-hued landscape.

North Window Arch and Turret Arch vie for attention in the Windows Section of Arches National Park.

PHOTOS: GLENN BAMBURG

Left, ***Visitors cross the stream near Wolfe Ranch on the trail to Delicate Arch, one of the many rewarding hikes in the park.*** **Right,** ***Other visitors enjoy panoramic views of the rugged range.***

"the toughest town in Utah." Today, it is a city extending a warm welcome to those visitors who appreciate the surrounding scenic beauty.

The entrance to Arches National Park appears soon after crossing the smoothly flowing Colorado River north of Moab on U.S. Highway 191. A visitors center offers maps and other publications, along with a color-slide program, a history exhibit and a geology museum explaining how the forces of wind, rain and frost have shaped the massive stone rainbows.

A self-guided driving tour coordinated with numbered stops along the paved road includes many points of interest, but to fully grasp the impressive scope of nature's handiwork, you may want to hike some of the shorter trails within the park.

The eighty plus natural arches and countless spires and towers have eroded over hundreds of millions of years. Park Avenue, which should be the first stop on your tour, features sandstone formations resembling a city skyline. In the area of the Courthouse Towers, there is evidence that arches of gigantic proportions have formed and already collapsed among the huge monolithic rocks.

Along the 23½-mile route are petrified sand dunes and a 55-foot Balanced Rock perched on a 73-foot pedestal. From the Windows Section, four large arches can be seen from the roadway. A short walk brings a closer view of Double Arch, whose awesome scale is difficult to imagine unless standing beneath the 163 by 157-foot span.

Farther along the route, an unpaved road leads to the remnants of Wolfe Ranch, which are partially hidden in a small valley on the banks of a meandering stream. Built in 1888 by a Civil War veteran, the log cabin and root cellar enabled us to turn back the pages of history to the time John Wolfe braved the remote region to eke out a meager existence.

From the parking area at the ranch, a 1½-mile footpath winds upward to the grand spectacle of Delicate Arch. Though the trail is somewhat taxing at several points, the rewarding view of the most photographed arch in the world is well worth the effort. Another view of Delicate Arch, etched against Utah's blue sky, can be seen from below, where the road continues to a smaller parking area. With a little imagination, it is easy to understand why early-day cowboys nicknamed this arch "schoolmarm's bloomers."

Returning to the paved road to continue our tour, we were enthralled by a dramatic overview of exposed sandstone fins, dubbed the Fiery Furnace. During the spring and summer months, two-hour hikes are led by rangers through the maze of stone walls, which cannot be entered without an experienced guide. These formations are often illuminated by a fiery orange glow at sunset, hence the unusual name.

Beyond the Fiery Furnace is Devil's Garden Campground, offering fifty tent and trailer sites with water and flush rest rooms available from early spring to first frost. During the winter months water is unavailable, but the park service does provide chemical toilets.

Past the campground entrance is the trailhead to the longest natural arch in the world. A twenty-minute walk will take you to the graceful, 300-foot span of Landscape Arch. From here, the trail continues on to Dark Angel and other arches, but hikers are warned that the terrain becomes more difficult to traverse. An adequate supply of water should be carried during the warmer months since there is no water along the trail.

Retracing our route to the visitors center and U.S. Highway 191, we turned north for five miles and then west on State Highway 313. Our next stop, Dead Horse Point State Park, is one of Utah's most unusual parks.

The panoramic view from Dead Horse Point State Park displays tier upon tier of towering sandstone cliffs standing guard on either side of the winding Colorado River, flowing 2,000 feet below. The 7,000-acre park received its name from one of the many timeworn legends of the West.

PHOTOS: GLENN BAMBURG

Top, *Wolfe Ranch was built in 1888 by a Civil War veteran; only remnants remain today.* Center, *Motorhomers catch their breath at Balance Rock, which seems about to fall from its sandstone pedestal.* Bottom, *Rafting enthusiasts challenge the Colorado River.*

Around the turn of the century, numerous herds of wild horses roamed the area of Utah near Moab. They could be seen sweeping across the desertlike terrain that was every bit as untamed and magnificent as the mustangs themselves. With heavy manes and untrimmed tails flying in the wind, they would flee into the vast reaches of canyons and rugged flats—prize catches for those daring cowboys who attempted their capture. To corral the spirited animals, the toughened wranglers utilized natural holding sites. One of these was a wide promontory of stone jutting out above the Colorado River. A narrow neck, thirty yards wide, was controlled with a makeshift fence of split rails, serving the cowboys' purpose successfully.

Herds of wild mustangs were driven out onto the high peninsula and the entrance secured by the quickly erected fence. Here, the better-quality steeds were roped and broken, either for selling to eastern markets or for the men's personal use. Unwanted horses or "broomtails," as they were called, were left on the point with the rail gate open, allowing them to regain their precious freedom on the range.

One group of rejects, however, is said to have been left without means of escape. Through some mistake, the rail fence was left in place and the herd of broomtails perished from thirst on this point far above the Colorado River.

A visitors center provides information, exhibits and a self-guided nature trail. The park is open all year; a developed campground is available from April through October. There are twenty-one units with modern rest rooms, covered picnic tables, electrical hookups and sewage dump stations. Winter camping is allowed on the point near the fenced overlook. Water is still a precious commodity at Dead Horse Point State

Park, and wise conservation is requested by park rangers.

Returning once again to Moab, a drive of unequalled scenic beauty awaits along State Route 128, northeast of the city. This highway parallels the Colorado River for thirty-five miles, flanked by sheer cliffs on one side and the majestic river on the other.

From the main route, a short side trip on a rather rough dirt road takes you to the dark-red spires of Fisher Towers. These 900-foot formations have been seen in numerous movies and television commercials.

Another paved road diverts from State Route 128 through the serene loveliness of Castle Valley, climbing upward through the Manti-La Sal National Forest and into the La Sal Mountains. Aside from panoramic views of Castle Valley, the far-reaching Canyonlands and Moab, the La Sal Mountain Loop Road is an unwinding tale of history. Along the sixty-one-mile route are two ghost-town sites, Pinhook Battleground and a mass grave for eight men ambushed by renegade Indians in 1881.

In the heart of the La Sals, Warner Lake is a beautiful retreat, excellent for picnicking and camping. Campsites, picnic tables, fresh water and toilets are surrounded by large aspen trees. Also offering camping facilities is Oowah Lake, located in the same vicinity. A high-clearance vehicle is recommended, but not absolutely necessary, to reach this lake.

For additional information concerning the above-mentioned guided driving tours and other area attractions, inquire at the visitors center located at 805 North Main in Moab, or contact Arches National Park, c/o Canyonlands National Park, Moab, Utah 84532, and/or Dead Horse Point State Park, Park Superintendent, P.O. Box 609, Moab, Utah 84532.

We have merely brushed the surface of nature's fine craftsmanship that abounds in the Moab region. The hidden sites waiting to be explored and admired are as numerous as the years involved in the creation of these scenic wonders. It is a land where time continues to leisurely carve and mold the earth to suit its own purpose, and one that requires ample time for viewing.

A Slice in Time

Oregon's incredible gorge has changed little since Lewis and Clark's challenging exploration

Jan Gumprecht Bannan

PHOTOS: JAN GUMPRECHT BANNAN

Wind surfers add color along the Columbia at Hood River Marina Park.

Several years ago I was fortunate enough to drive through the Columbia River Gorge in the early morning. I was greeted with one of those rare, seductive sunrises when the mist was breaking up as the sun pierced and melted its visibility. I was given—as gifts of beauty—peeks at rocky pinnacles and walls rising straight and royally near the side of the road, with a different waterfall plunging down every few minutes. Lichen-smeared rocky surfaces alternated with woods of lush, fern-hugged conifers that hinted of cool walks. Ridges slid into the river, daring it to devour them. In my mind's eye, I saw a Chinook Indian poised on a rock near the river, spear over his head, waiting for a salmon.

The images that lay before me changed frequently and held me captive with their intensity. Would you believe my camera was malfunctioning? I still enjoyed the sensual visual feast.

I returned with three cameras this year. It wasn't the same; it never is, but it was still good. White clouds slid in patterns over a punctured blue sky and skittered along ridge tops as I boarded the 145-foot sternwheeler *Columbia Gorge* at the Cascade Locks National Historic Site in

Highest in the gorge area, Multnomah lower and upper falls total 620 feet.

Oregon. Many early pioneers, traveling by stern-wheeler, first saw this gorge that was sliced through the erupting Cascade Mountains by the mighty Columbia River. Today's passengers don't have to furnish their own food and blankets, as some did back in 1850.

As we pulled away from the Marine Park, which, by the way, has a fine museum, I was drawn to the middle deck to watch the giant paddle wheel churning water and flashing a rainbow. Soon, however, the panorama of bisected mountains and river bends diverted me with a good perspective of the Columbia River Gorge—a superlative introduction.

Passing under the modern Bridge of the Gods, connecting Oregon and Washington, the two-hour narrated tour related the Indian legend of the earlier Bridge of the Gods, a natural rock formation, thought by geologists to have been built by a temporary landslide as late as 1260 A.D.

Time, the fourth dimension, presents changing vistas here, where water erosion pulverizes rock and washes it downstream. How long the gorge will be this spectacular is a question, but man has lived in the gorge area for at least 12,000 years and observed many geological developments.

I thought of Lewis and Clark and their joy—and then fear—at finding a river highway to the Pacific, but one interspersed with treacherous rapids and falls, and remnants of resistant rock in the gorge area. So infamous were these cascade rapids that the "mountains by the cascades" became known as the Cascade Range. In the year 1805, Lewis and Clark accepted the challenge of the Columbia Gorge and, with a combination of daring rides and lowering of boats with ropes, successfully maneuvered their way west.

The stern-wheeler *Harvest Queen* caused some excitement in 1890 when she shot the Cascade rapids. Today's stern-wheeler is a reminder of the importance of these boats in the past, when their arrival was an exciting event—bringing goods, news, a means of travel and the thrilling

PHOTO: JAN MIGLAVS

Crown Point appears through the mist of a clearing storm, adding an air of mystery to the timeless gorge.

entertainment of races among the stern-wheelers, with passengers cheering them on.

Top, *Many pioneers first saw the river via the stern-wheeler* **Harvest Queen**; *today's visitors travel on the* **Columbia Gorge**. Below, *On the scenic highway east of Mosier, Rowena Crest flowers in the spring.*

Today, the rapids and the famous fishing grounds of the Indians at Celilo Falls are no more. The Cascade Locks, built in 1896, were created for the passage of steamboat traffic. The Cascades of the Columbia were drowned by the Bonneville Dam in 1938, where my tour was docking. We turned around and paddled to Stevenson, Washington, passing platforms where Indians fish today, as Wind Mountain—home of the wind god—looms in the eastern distance.

PHOTOS: JAN GUMPRECHT BANNAN

Although RVers can see much from the stern-wheeler—and Interstate 84—the Columbia River Scenic Highway is the preferred route, and it is slower paced. The legislature appropriated $50,000 to build this road from Troutdale to The Dalles in 1872, but the work was not completed until 1916. For 37 years it was the only route through the Oregon portion of the Columbia Gorge. Today, two sections—the 22-mile loop from Troutdale to Ainsworth State Park and the nine-mile loop between Mosier and The Dalles—remain.

If your motorhome and you don't like negotiating narrow, winding roads, you can enter briefly at Corbett, Bridal Falls and Ainsworth. The most popular area, Multnomah Falls, can be seen from I-84 and the scenic highway. (In the past, trains brought passengers there.)

For a spectacular view of the gorge area and Crown Point Vista House—perched like a throne on this vertical cliff—stop at Chanticleer Lookout in Women's Forum State Park, less than two miles east of Corbett on the scenic highway, elevation 850 feet. A superb photographic landscape is seen from this elevated vista: The blue river with sandy bars are below. On the Washington side, farms of soft greens square off among the deep conifer greens. And to the east, coves and mountain ridges follow the weaving dance of the Columbia. Geology buffs can use the road guide from John Eliot Allen's book, *The Magnificent Gateway,* to orient themselves to the major features of the area.

What is most unusual about the Oregon side of the gorge are the waterfalls—the greatest concentration of high waterfalls in North America. The ice age and glaciation were the major factors in shaping the gorge area. Floods that followed—the first Bretz Flood had ten times the combined flow of all the rivers of the world—both scoured the gorge area and cut away the lower courses of tributary streams, and left high on the valley walls the hanging notches from which the falls descend.

Eleven falls over 100 feet high can be seen from I-84 or the scenic highway, and many more are not far away. Traveling east, past rainforest vegetation and dry masonry walls covered with moss, Latourell, Shepperd Dell State Park, Bridal Veil and Mist falls are easily visited. Wahkeena Falls, a multiple fall of 242 feet lined with golden flowers, and its famous neighbor, Multnomah Falls, offer a variety of photographic possibilities. Although much can be enjoyed even by wheelchair visitors, several interconnecting trails climb up the gorge to link these falls for good hiking. (Inquire at the Forest Service Information Center

Ainsworth State Park, near the crest of the gorge, is a good home base.

at Multnomah.) Highest in the gorge, the lower and upper falls of Multnomah are 620 feet high, with a bridge that crosses in between.

Oneonta Gorge offers a different kind of adventure for those who don't mind getting wet. A 900-foot trail up the stream bed—a gash between vertical walls—leads to Oneonta Falls.

This was a favorite loop of mine. I crossed the bridge over Oneonta Creek and watched the hikers negotiating the stream bed from the other side of Oneonta Gorge. Climbing a little, the trail wanders along a ridge with grand views of the Columbia River—take the scenic branch closer to the view—and then descends to circle a deep pool, passing under Upper Horsetail Falls, a beautiful, lush-green oasis, before going down to the road at Horsetail Falls.

Just west of Chanticleer, a good 14-mile road goes to the summit of 4,056-foot-high Larch Mountain. A 0.3-mile path leads to a view of five major peaks in the Cascades at Sherrard Point—a great place to watch sunsets on the Columbia River. Hiking trails go down the mountainside to connect with Horsetail and Multnomah falls.

Just past Horsetail Falls, good camping is available at Ainsworth State Park. Majestic Yakima basalt pinnacles rise near the forested sites. Only 37 miles east of Portland, the park has full hookups

East of Ainsworth, the scenic highway ends, but easy exits from I-84 are possible at Bonneville—to see how the dam operates and to see migrating fish—and at a Forest Service campground, Eagle Creek. Rest rooms are available, but no hookups.

Staying in the Eagle Creek area for several days, I hiked the beautiful, wooded Eagle Creek Trail along a ledge above the creek to Punch Bowl Falls and then to High Bridge. Another time I ascended the Wauna Viewpoint Trail—1.8 miles one way—for good views of the sparkling Columbia flowing west. Returning to the creek, I was surprised by a blue heron, who flew into the quiet woods next to me while I was cooling my feet in the blue-green water.

Another exit is at Cascade Locks. Portage Days, with a salmon feed and stern-wheeler run, are scheduled the second weekend in August. Cascade Locks offers a choice of two good campgrounds. One is in the Marina Park, near the stern-wheeler rides and the old lock. The other is on the outskirts of town near the river—Bridge of the Gods KOA. If the weather is hot, as happens frequently in the gorge area, and especially if I've been hiking some of the steep gorge trails, I enjoy the swimming pool at this campground. All the amenities are available, with roomy, wooded sites.

Farther east, at Hood River Marina Park, I discovered a good windsurfing region on the river, where international competitions are held. I spent a couple of days being a spectator at the pro-am, with contestants including Robby Naish from Hawaii. Camping is available at Viento State Park, eight miles west of Hood River, and Memaloose County Park, three miles east of Mosier.

Come visit the Columbia Gorge in spring, when wildflowers escort you up its trails, or in the warmth of summer, or to see the colors of autumn. And, if you are hardy, venture to Multnomah during a cold winter, when the falls are a sculpture of ice. Whenever you come, I think you, too, will call it beautiful.

California Suite

Witness the marvels of Joshua Tree National Monument, where Mother Nature orchestrates a colorful springtime production

Doug Emerson

PHOTOS: DOUG EMERSON

Spectacular ocotillo blossoms adorn tips of long, heavily spiked branches.

Every spring, we motorhome to some desert destination to observe the miracle that Mother Nature creates. When the rains reach the dried earth, everything is transformed, the previously barren wasteland becomes one of the world's most spectacularly beautiful spots. During the past 40 years, our favorite desert destination has become Joshua Tree National Monument in Southern California, a vast area with literally hundreds of good camping sites.

The monument straddles two great American deserts: the Mojave, to the north, rising to nearly 5000 feet above sea level, and the lesser-known Colorado, a subdivision of the Sonoran Desert, dipping to a little over 1,000 feet in the south.

Although there's not a great distance between the two, the difference in elevation accounts for the variety of plants and animals that have adapted to these localities.

During many springtime visits we have photographed huge Joshua trees that reached 40 feet into the sky, spreading their grotesque, hairy arms in all directions. At the other extreme, tiny belly-flowers, so small we use a macro lens to obtain pictures of these dainty desert dwellers,

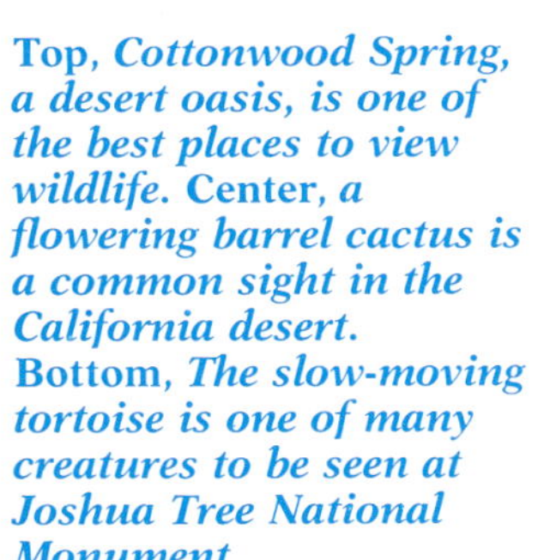

Top, ***Cottonwood Spring, a desert oasis, is one of the best places to view wildlife.*** **Center,** ***a flowering barrel cactus is a common sight in the California desert.*** **Bottom,** ***The slow-moving tortoise is one of many creatures to be seen at Joshua Tree National Monument.***

with blooms often less than 1/8 inch in diameter.

In many areas, great concentrations of wildflowers, exhibiting colors that would put any self-respecting rainbow to shame, raised havoc with our film supply, but caused Kodak stockholders to rub their hands in glee.

During good years, when the usually parched desert is blessed with sufficient water at the proper time, the transformation is breathtaking, a never-to-be-forgotten spectacle. Dozens of varieties, from white through greens, yellows, pinks through varying shades of orange and red to purple, are good reasons to return to the desert year after year. Depending upon elevation, we have found excellent wildflowers from March through May. The higher the elevation, the later the flowers bloom.

One of the most amazing relationships is that between the yucca moth and the Joshua tree (and most other yuccas). Whereas most pollinating occurs accidentally, this female moth deliberately collects pollen, which she spreads on the receptive surface of the flower. No other insect performs such an act. However, she has a selfish purpose in mind, that of perpetuating her species. She lays her eggs in the flower's ovary, so the resultant larva will have seeds to eat. To reciprocate for this, the considerate larva eats only a few of the many seeds, leaving the rest to bounce across the landscape before establishing residence. This accounts for widespread groves of the unusual trees.

Look at the dried seed pods, and you will note tiny holes in each one. No seeds can develop without having been visited by the female moth. One could not live without the other, yet, strangely, the moth receives no direct benefit from her labors. She eats neither pollen nor nectar, as other pollinators do. Mother Nature is wonderful, isn't she?

Another tree, the unusual palo verde, with green trunk and branches, is completely covered with beautiful yellow blooms in spring.

But perhaps the most spectacular sight in the monument is the Cholla

The silhouette of a spindly ocotillo at sunset entrances a lone hiker.

Garden, when thousands of bristling plants are backlighted in late evening. These notorious "jumping cactus," do not actually jump to attack anyone venturing too close. It is the unwary individual who does the actual jumping. The spines are so friendly they will attach themselves to anything they contact, whether lying on the ground or still on the plant. Adults should be very cautious, especially if there are children or pets present. Should a spine fasten itself to any part of your clothing, shoes or skin, do *not* attempt to pick it off. Use a stick, screwdriver, pliers or anything but your fingers to remove it.

Oddly, pack rats use these formidable, spiny building blocks to construct homes that afford them ample protection from predators. You will notice many of these cozy little mansions among the cholla plants.

The Ocotillo Patch, a bit farther on, is a startling sight, especially when fiery little blooms grace the long, heavily thorned branches at the tips. This plant is not a cactus, in spite of the thorns.

Folks who have never seen a smoke tree will be able to see how it got its name by observing dozens of them in washes on both sides of the road heading south.

Few visitors will be fortunate enough to see such creatures as desert bighorn sheep, mule deer or mountain lion. These larger animals

PHOTO: GEORGE OSTERTAG

learned long ago that people cannot be trusted.

Members of the animal kingdom that most visitors to Joshua Tree do see are the tiny antelope ground squirrels. They aren't at all bashful about accepting food, with little regard for where the food stops and fingers begin. For this reason, among others, it is unwise and illegal to feed animals in any unit of the national park system. Besides, they will get along much better without our well-intentioned help.

Black-tailed jackrabbits are common, but much more aloof, preferring to maintain a sensible distance from all people. Maybe their memory banks tell them that human beings like rabbit stew.

With care, you can approach them and, with luck, observe the sun shining through the huge, erect, almost transparent ears. Jackrabbits, by the way, are not rabbits at all, but hares, acquiring their common name by association with jackasses.

Occasionally a coyote will allow itself to be photographed, a thrilling sight for some visitors. Their "crooning" at night and in early morning hours often sends cold chills coursing through bodies of those unaccustomed to the eerie sound. We enjoy listening to them, mainly because it is definite evidence that these clever wild creatures have not become extinct, as have so many others during the past century.

The bounding kangaroo rat is often seen at night, seemingly leaping with wild abandon, apparently trying to exceed the last prodigious distance. Its ability to live an entire lifetime without a drink of water is astounding. Being able to manufacture needed moisture from dry seeds is but one more example of how Mother Nature has endowed her creatures for survival.

That always-in-a-hurry member of the cuckoo clan, the road runner, is probably the most common bird visitors see here. Known as the clown of the desert, with a tail longer than the rest of its body, it is capable of flying, but prefers to live up to its name. It darts about, seeking a tasty morsel in the form of an unwary lizard or snake, attacking with amazing speed to deliver the coup de grâce. Poisonous or not, it makes little difference to this persistent predator as it grabs a streaking lizard while both are in floorboarded overdrive.

Despite their lightning like strikes, many rattlesnakes, especially the diminutive sidewinder, become a favorite meal for these fearless birds. With blazing speed, they dart to attack, then retreat, just out of reach. Apparently their computerized measuring device is amazingly accurate. Quite often, unless the snake is able to retreat into a hole or under a protective bush, it gets pecked to death.

We have located many road runner nests cleverly hidden among seemingly impenetrable cholla bushes. How the adults and young manage to avoid the needle-sharp barbs has always baffled us.

You may visit the desert many times and never see or hear any member of the rattlesnake clan. They seem to fear people as much as people fear them.

Lizards seem to know they can outrun us without even breathing hard. Maybe this is why they will often allow someone with a camera to approach slowly, then they scamper away as if an imaginary line has been overstepped.

Horned toads, which are actually lizards, are a bit easier to grab. They probably wonder why we aren't frightened when they squirt a fine stream of blood from the nictitating membrane of their eyes to a distance of several feet. Once they realize we mean them no harm, they seem to relax and enjoy a gentle stroking under the chin. When we return them to the ground, these ferocious-appearing, yet harmless miniature dragons streak for the nearest bush.

The giant Parry Nolina in Hidden Valley at Joshua Tree National Monument towers over a visitor.

Desert tortoises are much less mobile. Not designed for speed, they will reluctantly pose for pictures before ambling away, looking back resentfully, as they seek a succulent bit of native vegetation. Don't try to rub one under the chin, no matter how friendly you feel at the time. You may immediately and painfully discover you no longer have the same number of fingers as before the encounter.

Camping amidst boulders and native plants is a perfect way to enjoy the beauty of Joshua Tree National Monument.

PHOTOS: DOUG EMERSON

Access to the most visited portions of the monument is via either Joshua Tree or Twentynine Palms on State Highway 62 or, from the south, off Interstate 10/U.S. 60. For first-time visitors, we highly recommend entry via Oasis Visitors Center, from Twentynine Palms that offers a nice cactus garden, interesting displays and an informative slide program.

There are about 500 campsites, most suitable for all but the largest rigs, in Black Rock and Indian Cove campgrounds, the latter between Joshua Tree and Twentynine Palms.

Although not shown on many state maps, Black Rock Canyon Campground is an excellent all-year facility with 100 gravel sites among strange-looking Joshua trees. There's a dump station, as well as flush toilets, and the campsites can accommodate practically any size motorhome. It is reached by paved Joshua Lane off State Highway 62.

For those who prefer the amenities of a private campground, several are available in the vicinity. Consult the *1989 Trailer Life Campground & RV Services Directory* for additional campgrounds.

Once you have visited this interesting Southern California monument in the beautiful springtime, you are sure to return, as we have, to discover something startlingly different and worthwhile every time.

Desert Christ Park

Sculptured figures of Christ and children are among many lifesize pieces carved by Antone Martin in Yucca Valley.

Several years ago we were astounded by the sight of a huge figure of Christ, the almost pure-white likeness standing out boldly against a deep-blue desert sky.

Located in a Bibical-type setting, a hillside overlooking Yucca Valley, California, all but two of the more than 30 lifesize or larger statues are the work of one man, Antone Martin.

Desert Christ Park is a truly unique collection of solid concrete statuary, designed and sculptured by Martin and dedicated to all humanity, to be viewed without charge at all hours, every day of the year.

Originally called Hi-Desert Shrine Park, the name was changed to its present title when presented to Yucca Valley Park and Recreation District for perpetuity.

Antone Martin, artist-sculptor, lived on the site from 1953 until his death in 1961. His last few years were devoted exclusively to creating the snow-white statuary, ranging from life-size to 12-feet tall, weighing from 4 to 16 tons.

The most impressive Last Supper facade, which dominates the entire area, is three stories high and weighs an estimated 125 tons. Placed around a 30-foot-long table, the 13 figures are bigger than life.

Carved in bas-relief, except for the three-dimensional head of Christ before the open window, the work is indeed a masterpiece.

An inspiring group of 9-foot-tall individualized figures represent the Sermon on the Mount, featuring Christ and his disciples.

Even those with no particular religious belief can appreciate the immensity of the project and the many hours of dedicated effort that went into it, with no thought of reward other than the satisfaction of completing a task that the sculptor sincerely believed in.

Antone Martin gave up a high-salary position as a skilled senior pattern maker at an aircraft plant to retire to this desert community, where he could give expression—in a concrete way—to his convictions. Well beyond retirement age, Martin created the figures, using only voluntary contributions from anyone who wished to make them and a large portion of his retirement income to make his dream become a reality.

Located on State Highway 62 (often referred to as Twentynine Palms Highway), Yucca Valley is easily accessible from Interstate 10/U.S. 60. It is about 125 miles due east of Los Angeles and about 30 miles north of Palm Springs.

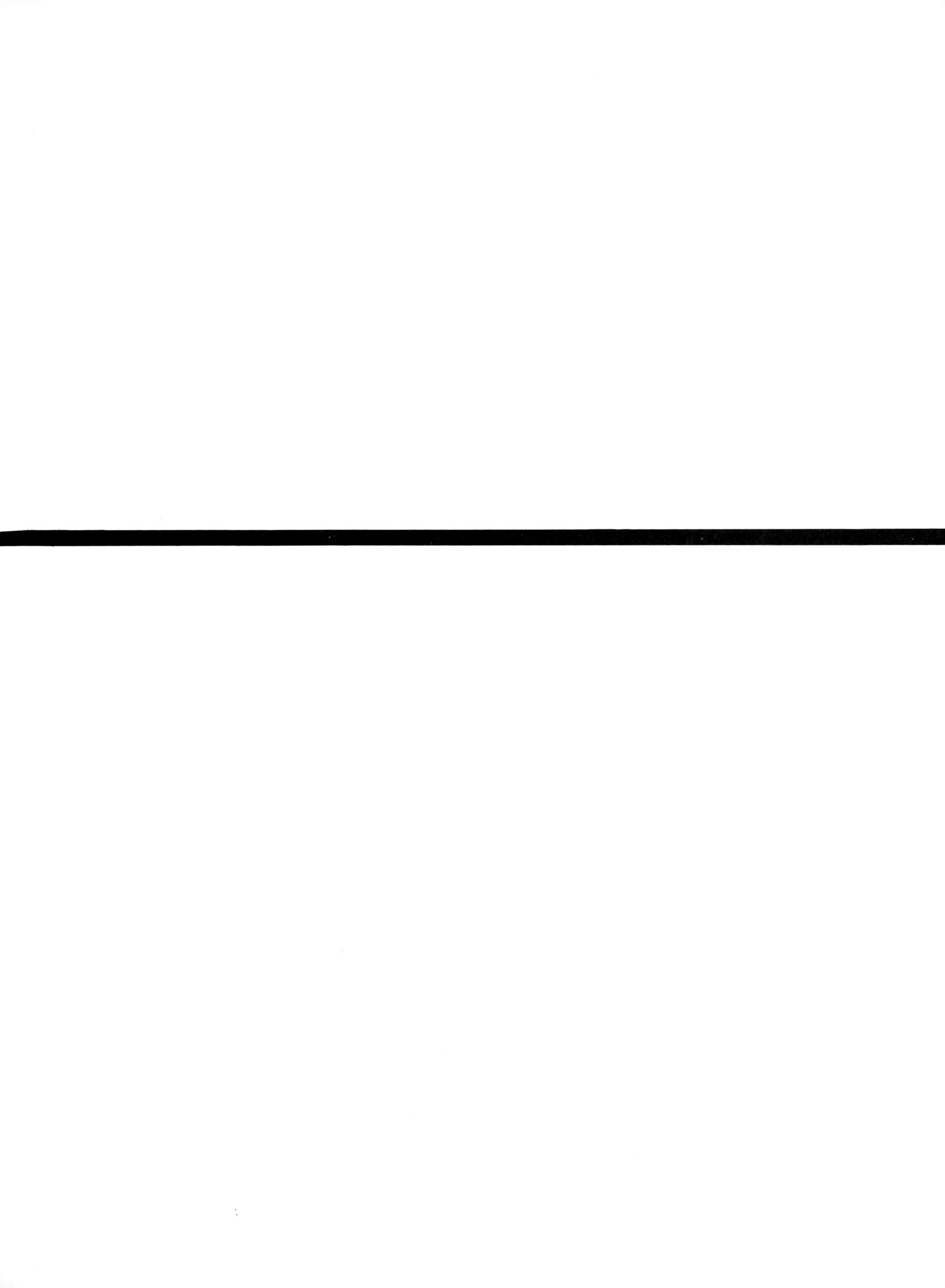

FOREIGN LANDS

The Baja Experience

A true motorhome adventure awaits spirited travelers on this primitive Mexican peninsula

Fred Hoctor

Afternoon siestas are a fact of life in the sunny, slow-paced country of Mexico, and hammocks are ideal for taking them.

PHOTO: FRED HOCTOR

An attractive young couple from Paris, piloting a dusty old Land Rover camper on a 'round-the-world odyssey, rapped at my door in northern Baja the other day to ask for local directions. They had just spent a week negotiating the astonishing, 1,000-mile, sinuous desert highway from Cabo San Lucas to Ensenada.

"We had read about it in all the European travel magazines," gushed the awe-stricken Frenchman, "and now that we have seen it, we still cannot believe it. Africa, Asia, the Orient . . . nothing is quite like it. This thing cannot be *real.*"

It is this chimerical, dreamlike quality which, above all else, flags Baja as one of the greatest of North America's RV adventures.

Baja California, a rugged, sparsely inhabited peninsula longer than Italy, is primitive, raw and as much frozen in time as a gasp-inducing Ansel Adams photograph of the Tetons. Baja is big sky and endless trails, picturesque Alpine meadows, savage mountains tumbling to the sea, heart-stopping turquoise lagoons, sultry, many-palmed oases and undulant, surreal desert, stretching away forever.

But Baja is also bustling border-town honky-tonks, languorous isolated villages and remote seaside fishing camps. Posh world-class resort hotels rise ethereally from the shimmering desert sands, seemingly in the middle of nowhere. The land is arid, tropical and arid again, and

PHOTO: PAUL PIERCE

Baja's old road was a supreme challenge; today's highway has made the trek safer and easier, but still rugged enough to suit adventurers.

the sometimes-tortured landscape, forbidding yet eerily inviting, is often so out of whack with reality that the discrepancy can disorient and overwhelm the tenderfoot.

Since the opening of the narrow, peninsula-long highway little more than a decade ago, I have watched my Baja change. I am neither nostalgic nor wistful about this because most of the changes have been only in the vicinity of the highway itself, and they have made Baja considerably safer, more accessible and convenient for travelers. But if you come to Baja anticipating an American-type excursion, with manicured campgrounds at every turn, drive-in theaters and frequent stops at convenience stores or fast-food restaurants, prepare yourself for a surprise.

Baja is the real thing. As if to prove this, it is a curious fact that none of man's inventions works in Baja. The hot-water faucet nearly always delivers cold, while the cold faucet, though turned on fully, invariably drips lukewarm. If you see this as inconvenient rather than charming, don't come.

And leave your wristwatch at home. It will not keep proper time in Baja, anyway. The Baja day is 48 hours long. Rise and bed down with the sun, taking a midday break for siesta, and you will experience this mysterious "double-day" phenomenon for yourself. A week's vacation will seem like two, two like four, etc. The pace of living, compared even to small-town America's, is tantalizingly slow.

If you miss a single sunrise while in Baja, legend says your heart has skipped a beat. The dazzling dawn is especially spectacular on the Sea of Cortés in late spring, summer and fall, often turning that translucent, 700-mile-long marvel of water to the incredible hue of a Thai ruby; sunsets, or *crepusculos*, can transmigrate from orange to scarlet to deep purple within half an hour, and they are noble times, celebrated for themselves. "Can you come for a sunset?" is a common party invitation from San Felipe to Cabo San Lucas.

Is Baja safe? So much nonsense has been written about Baja by gee-

PHOTO: EMIL BARJAK

A local fishing boat is stranded at low tide near San Felipe.

Green Angels roam the highway to assist travelers in distress; this unique service is the world's largest such security network and is run by the Ministry of Tourism.

PHOTOS: PAUL PIERCE

whiz journalists that we who live here often chuckle at the outpourings. Yet little has been written about the special tricks that make Baja travel not only viable, but an unforgettable experience for RVers of all ages. Baja is as safe as you make it. But just as you should not go to sea without a compass, you should not essay the Baja experience without knowing and following the unique rules that apply here.

First, do not venture into the unknown "seas" of Baja without proper "charts." The most important of these, for first-timers, is an inexpensive but updated road log, which should be available from the company that provides your Mexican insurance.

Mexican insurance coverage is somewhat expensive, but without it, in the event of an accident, you will be detained until fault is established by a local judge—not a pleasant procedure. If you are bringing a boat, a utility vehicle or a sport vehicle, be sure that it, too, is insured. And do not rely on your U.S. insurance to cover you. Mexican insurance can be purchased at any of several companies near the U.S. side of the border, or at a small building on the right, just after crossing the border at Tijuana.

Although there are many insurance companies offering Mexican coverage, two that are recommended are Instant Mexico Auto Insurance, 223 Via de San Ysidro, San Ysidro, California 92073, (619) 428-4714; and Sanborn's, Department T, Box 1210, McAllen, Texas 78501, (512) 682-3401. Contacting one of these offices before departure will provide you with plenty of information as well as a road log that offers up-to-date road conditions, trailer parks and other facilities.

If you have a serious disability or a potential for catastrophic illness, it might be wise to call International Air-Evac, a San Diego-based firm that operates both land and air ambulance service out of Baja to stateside hospitals in case of emergency. The number is (619) 292-5557. While clinics are found in the major villages along the highway, the only reliable Baja hospitals are in the north, at Tijuana and Ensenada.

There is a famous song in Mexico called "The Fishermen of Ensenada." Its heart-wrenching plaint: "Many go out, but few return."

I have long threatened to borrow the line for a paean to travelers on the Baja Highway, that narrow ribbon of asphalt laid ever so gently on the shifting sands of one of the world's most rugged deserts. Highway engineers snicker at the impermanence of Mexico 1D, its lack of foundation and its mute hostility to the thousands of overladen RVs that travel its length every year. Yet an army of *trabajadores* (workmen), flailing away with pick and shovel, have been able to keep this world-

A flash flood can be the Baja traveler's greatest foe; there is little warning before roads turn into rivers, sometimes stranding vehicles for days.

famous road somewhat intact despite heat, floods and windstorms that constantly threaten to whisk it into perdition at any moment.

The makeshift, wind-rippled and rock-bedeviled sand roads that augment this single north-south pavement are even worse, of course, and unless you are in superb physical condition, thoroughly understand desert driving, and have enough tools, know-how and spare parts to rebuild your vehicle from the ground up, my advice is to avoid all of them when driving a motorhome. Unfortunately, many of the most inviting RV areas are a mile or more from the highway—San Lucas Cove (1 mile), Punta Chivato (14 miles) and most of the gorgeous western Concepción Bay parks (up to a mile) come immediately to mind—and even these rough approach roads can be tough on your rig.

Knowing from experience that most RVers are magnetically drawn to the challenge of such terrain, that more and more motorhomers are bringing offroad vehicles to Baja, and having driven nearly half a million Baja miles myself, I offer these humble suggestions:

Even if you don't know a wrench from a hammer, carry a good general-purpose set of tools, a shovel and a stout tow rope. At every turn in the road there is a smiling Mexican fellow who knows what each is for.

Don't attempt the most inviting road, even with four-wheel-drive, until you have definitely identified it on a *recent* map and checked locally to be sure it is passable for your particular vehicle. The road may look okay where it leaves the highway, then dwindle off into a nightmare of cactus and boulders, with no turnaround. If your informant speaks no English, you can usually make your inquiry understood with sign language. If somewhere in his response you hear the word *malo,* don't try the road. Malo (bad) is a very serious word in Baja.

During the summer rainy season in the south and the winter season in the north, you will have to be especially watchful for chuckholes and detours on the main highway and flash floods on side roads. Both can end your trip permanently. The best source for up-to-the-minute road conditions is Gina Cord at the Baja Information Bureau in San Diego—(619) 295-3374. Even if Gina's report is glowing, however, you will want to prepare for really heavy-duty travel.

Now, when and where do you go?

Though the very best months for travel are May and October, keep in mind that Mexico Highway 1D, which meanders back and forth across the peninsula, is about the same length as the highway between Philadelphia and Miami, covering an equally wide variance in climate. While it is unbearably hot on the Gulf side in summer months, there is nearly always good weather somewhere on the peninsula at any given time of the year. Even in summer, Punta Banda, 20 miles south of Ensenada, has moderate weather and plentiful RV facilities. And except for occasional *chubascos* (tropical storms), the stunning resort area of Los Cabos, far to the south, with six good RV parks, has delightful weather from fall to spring.

Native fishermen continue to use the simplest of crafts in the time-honored way.

PHOTO: EMIL BARJAK

Baja's main-highway gas stations are like the stagecoach stops of old. They are centers for gossip and news. If you don't like the weather where you are, drive to the nearest station and ask the travelers coming from both directions what the weather conditions were up or down the line. Don't be timid. You'll find a surprising camaraderie among Baja travelers. The big advantage to this, of course, is that your information will be current and you will not have to rely on generalized and uncertain weather reports.

For many years, the major problem with Baja travel has been the quality and availability of gasoline. A Baja-wise petroleum chemist I know claims that Mexican regular (Nova) could be as low as 68 octane on our rating system, a cut above kerosene. You will probably have to retard your timing slightly and add a top oil/gas booster like Bardahl or STP to your tank. I have found that a new product, TK-7, works especially well at reducing knocks and is highly concentrated so that I need to take along only a few bottles instead of a carton.

The unleaded (Extra) is not much better than Nova, and with most engines requires similar precautions. Unlike Nova, Extra is becoming *decreasingly* available outside of major cities, though by filling up at every PEMEX station where it is available, you can go the length of the peninsula without resorting to regular.

Prices for both grades have fluctuated so dramatically with recent succeeding peso devaluations, that there is no sense even guessing what you will have to pay, though it will probably be 10 percent to 20 percent less than U.S. prices. Diesel costs as much as 50 percent less than in the States and is available almost every place you find Nova.

All three fuels are likely to be dirty, so be sure your filters are clean and ready for action. I recommend adding an extra filter on the fuel line above the tank, for added safety.

Another factor that obviates using as little Mexican gas as possible is that because of temperature fluctuations and the resulting condensation, there's likely to be water in the gas, even though cement—that's right, *cement*—is used as a stabilizer. This may not be catastrophic for your RV engine, but it can be murder on 2-cycle engines. Outboards using Mexican gas sometimes have to have concrete chipped off the vents and often quit at sea because of fouled plugs or water in the gas.

PHOTO: FRED HOCTOR

Swimming is great in the clear waters near Los Cabos, where the Pacific meets the Sea of Cortez at Baja's southern tip.

What is the solution to all this? Bring as much gas from the United States as possible, and if you have to stretch it out, mix it half and half with the Mexican gas. Even a few gallons of good gas per tank goes a long way.

There is no unleaded gasoline available at Bahía de Los Angeles.

Never use plastic gas containers in Baja. Because of the strong sun, the jarring and the frequent pressure induced by heat expansion of the gasoline, the plastic tends to deteriorate rapidly, and I have seen plastic seams burst wide open. Instead, get high-quality, heavy-gauge metal cans made specifically for gasoline storage and secure them firmly with mounts and straps. Never mount these in the front of the vehicle or on the left (traffic) side, and only on the right side or top if you have to. It is a lot of expense, but the Baja way is to mount them on a sturdy dock bumper at the stern, framed within a 2-inch roll bar in case of a collision from behind. Some Southern California dealers specialize in installing permanent auxiliary "Baja tanks," which hold up to 100 gallons. It should be said that many Bajaphiles have made successful trips the length of the highway and back relying totally on Mexican gas, but my advice is to baby your engine as much as possible with higher-octane U.S. gas if you can.

Pre-mixed outboard gas can be used in your vehicle in a pinch, but if you use more than 10 gallons or so, I can tell you from long experience that, in time, it will foul your plugs. In any case, definitely carry an extra set of points and plugs as well as an extra air filter, as local shops carry limited selections.

Much has happened in Baja in recent years. Many new trailer parks, too numerous to mention, have sprung up along the highway, and the availability of ice, fuel and bottled water is far more reliable than ever before. Even the famous "out-of-order" gas pumps at La Prieta, the midpeninsula turnoff to the beautiful Bahía de Los Angeles, are now equipped with an emergency generator, hopefully ending the long lines of motorists waiting for power to be restored after the frequent blackouts in this remote area. Ice, groceries, water and fuel are available now at Ensenada, San Quintín, Bahía de Los Angeles, Guerrero Negro, Mulegé, Loreto, La Paz, Los Cabos and many other points along the way. However, it is always a good idea to top off your tanks whenever they get below half full, as delivery of fuel to individual stations is sometimes iffy, particularly over big holiday weekends.

Going south, you will nearly always find gas at Guerrero Negro. Going north, if you get as far as Cataviñá and still find no gas, here is a secret: There is an airstrip just to the south of Cataviñá, one mile off of the road at Josefina's Rancho Santa Ynez. Watch for the paved side road and a sign on the east side of the highway. Fred, the ranch foreman, will sometimes sell you some airplane gas—if he has plenty and if you look desperate enough. Otherwise, I advise waiting at the Cataviñá PEMEX station until gas is delivered. (Get in line.)

Do not, under *any* conditions, drive any part of the highway at night, as it is extremely narrow, poorly lit, sometimes pocked with chuckholes and often blocked by inexplicable, nearly invisible detour barriers or wandering cows. My fishing companion, Miguel Lopez Lopez, claims that in Baja the cow is god. "On the highway," says Miguel, "only the cow decides whether you live or die." For that reason, take it easy on speed even in the daytime; 50 mph is plenty, less in areas where there are curves *(curvas)* and dips *(vados)*.

If you should run out of gas or have a breakdown on the highway in a remote area, do not leave your vehicle. Get it well off the road, if you can, and wait for help. The help will usually come in the form of a Green Angel *(Angel Verde)*, one of a fleet of green emergency trucks that patrol the entire length of the highway every day, the first tourist service of its kind in the world. If one of the trucks is nearby, you can sometimes reach its driver on CB emergency channel 9, though you will probably get help just as fast by simply waiting awhile. Carry a special "help" sign for such emergencies. If you leave your vehicle unattended, it might be looted, and you will get little sympathy from police.

PHOTO: EMIL BARJAK

PHOTO: FRED HOCTOR

Top, *Open-air vegetable markets show Baja's natural bounty, which is safe to eat if washed carefully first.* Bottom, *Bullfighting, Mexico's favorite entertainment, is also popular with tourists.*

In the summer, especially, be certain that your hoses and belts are in top condition and carry spares. I have found that a roll of duct tape and heavy wire can be great allies. The main parts-and-repair areas south of Tijuana are located in Ensenada, Guerrero Negro and La Paz, but if you get in trouble out on the highway, the Green Angels patrol units will sometimes be able to jerry-rig something for you or, at the least, bring you the parts you need within a day. If the problem is a broken axle or an equivalent disaster, stay with your vehicle until a Green Angel shows up, then let *him* tell you the best solution. There may be a hidden welding shop (*soldadura*) just behind the next sand dune.

If you are off the main highway, of course, you are at the mercy of your own ingenuity and mechanical ability, and it is on the backroads that you are most likely to get in trouble. Do not take such a possibility lightly. People die of thirst on these deserts trying to walk five miles to the highway. Few of these roads are suitable for motorhomes anyway.

In short, this is serious, big-time wilderness country, and taking a side road for a lark is foolish. There is enough to worry about on the main highway, which in most places is only about 20 feet wide. In one place, which I measured the other day, the width was exactly 17 feet 9 inches, and there were no shoulders to speak of. Two 8-foot-wide motorhomes passing each other can be a squeaky affair at any point on the highway. You should be careful, too, of tight curves, especially those between San Ignacio and Santa Rosalía. These are usually steeply graded, and when a semi swings wide, there can be no place to go. Take all curves very, very slowly. Take it easy, too, where you see the warning sign *vado* (dip).

In high summer, temperatures can reach 110°F. When parked, find some way to provide shade for your refrigeration unit. There are especially good block-ice manufacturing plants at Ensenada, Mulegé and La Paz, and you can purchase cubes (*cubos*) at many stops along the way. Be sure to wash the ice well before using it in drinks, and stick to chilled soda pop or beer if you want to be extra safe. The Spanish word for ice is *hielo* (pronounced "yellow"). Watch for the signs.

Another sign to watch for is *llantera*. It means tire shop, and its operator is a *llantero* (pronounced yantero). These men can do wonders, but if you have done irreparable damage to a wheel or tire, don't go much farther without getting a new spare. Many highway-side *llanteros* carry a surprisingly wide selection of used tires, which should tell you something about the highway.

Lacking signs or flares, Mexicans often mark an accident, a crippled car or a detour with stones on the highway. Keep a sharp eye.

Never attempt the highway at all without the best suspension system you can put on your vehicle, not only for the sake of clearance and comfort, but because the highway, when badly pocked, simply eats up stock suspension systems. And a bad sway on a road this narrow can be a disaster.

It could be worth your life to have your brakes inspected before you leave on your Baja trip. There are some extra-steep grades, particularly in the mountains south of Ensenada, in the northern approach to the Vizcaíno Desert and again north of San Ignacio. Many of the crosses by the side of the road are memorials to victims of runaways. If your brakes start to pull, flutter or fade, stop as soon as possible at one of the repair centers.

If all this sounds like a nightmare, I hasten to assure you that the Baja Highway, driven safely and with the proper equipment, can be a pleasure. But I think too little has been written about its perils, particularly for big rigs. The result has been cocky driving, which can be trouble anywhere, but particularly here.

The big news in Baja is the new emergency-phone system on the 60-mile stretch of highway between Tijuana and Ensenada. The solar-powered SOS phones broadcast directly to a radio operator near the tollgate at the Playas Tijuana tourist information booth (where you can purchase a very good Baja map for about $1.50), and help can be dispatched immediately.

RV parks charge from $4 to $7 per night, and many have showers, hookups and laundry facilities. English is spoken nearly everywhere along the route, and all major facilities will accept American dollars, though you will usually save money by paying in pesos, which you can purchase at bargain rates in the currency-exchange offices at San Ysidro, just before entering Mexico. Do not buy more pesos than you think you can use, however, as they tend to devaluate very quickly lately, and overnight drops of 20 percent in value are not unknown.

Unless you are accompanied by a group of other RVers, my advice is to limit your trip to the major RV areas, where facilities are plentiful and you will be assured of some degree of security in the park you select. My favorites are Punta Banda on the Pacific side and Bahía de Los Angeles, Mulegé, Loreto, Buena Vista and Los Cabos on the Gulf. They all happen to be great fishing areas, and all can be reached without leaving paved roads. Remote and lonely desert beaches are tempting, but they also invite camp thieves, who are likely to walk off with anything from a loose can of beer to your favorite camera. This is especially true in the beach camps south of San Felipe, the Gringa Point area just north of Bahía de Los Angeles, the camping areas on the south end of Bahía de Concepción and, during the winter months, most of the beach areas that lie between Tijuana and Ensenada.

Is Baja full of thieves? Not especially. But there are some bad *hombres* here, just as there are in most places. It is always amazing to me to see people who triple-lock their doors at home, but who will leave a $100,000 motorhome unattended and wide open on a remote beach and go fishing for six hours with no thought of being robbed.

Take reasonable precautions, drive carefully, allow yourself plenty of time, and your Baja trip will be an incredible journey, in many places reminiscent of a movie set of the Old West, in others so breathtakingly beautiful that you may opt, as I did 30 years ago, to establish a permanent home here.

Baja has a lot of faults. The roads are not always in the best condition, it can get hot as blazes, and mechanical things don't seem to work at all. But one thing is certain: There is absolutely no place like it in the world. And once you have seen Baja, you will never forget it.

AN INSIDER'S TIPS

What to Wear

Winter: raingear, warm sweater, jacket, jumpsuit, hiking boots, tennis shoes, loafers, autumn-weight sport jacket, short-sleeve sport shirt, slacks, bathing suit, jeans, work shirt, golf hat.

Summer: shorts, bathing suit, light slacks or khakis, jeans, long-sleeve cotton shirt, wide-brimmed sun hat, golf hat, tennis shoes, thongs, loafers, hiking boots.

Bring good walking shoes for shopping, resort and camp wear to suit the season.

Special Buys

Kahlua liqueur, baskets, blankets, handicrafts, leather goods. Most convenient shopping: Ensenada.

First-Aid Kit Additions

Pepto Bismol, sunscreen, behind-the-ear prescription patches if you are prone to seasickness and plan to fish, insect repellent, tetracycline, deodorant bar soap.

Dish Soap

Only a salt-resistant, grease-cutting detergent like Vel or Joy will handle the water.

Food and Drink

Nearly all staples you will need are available at local stores, but bring along instant pancake mix, syrup, butter, margarine and dried potatoes. Wash all fruits and vegetables well. Drink only bottled water *(agua potable),* for sale even in the smallest village. In summer heat, avoid alcohol (it dehydrates you); canned peaches are a great thirst slaker; hot sun tea refreshes best. Baja bakery *(panadería)* items, often excellent and always inexpensive, include sweet rolls, tortes and cookies. Small bread loaves, baked daily without preservatives, are called *bolillos.* Deep-fried wedges of corn tortillas make good chips. Camp near fishermen and you will probably get all the fresh fish you want, free for the cleaning. Avoid fresh meats except in good restaurants and big-city markets. Don't eat anything from food stands. Irradiated, condensed milk *(leche en cartón)* is safest and keeps for over a month. Local Nescafé coffee is okay; Cafe d'Oro is great. The *limon* (lime) is king here, and Bajans use it on virtually everything. As for smokes, bring enough of your own brand to last the trip. American cigarettes are seldom available, although Havana cigars are.

Classic Baja Meals

Lobster at Puerto Nuevo, on the road adjacent to the Tijuana/Ensenada toll road; anything at El Rey Sol restaurant in Ensenada (French/Mexican); turtle steak at Casa Diaz, Bahía de Los Angeles; Saturday barbecue at Hotel Serenidad, Mulegé; buffet breakfast at El Presidente Hotel, Chateaubriand at Damiana restaurant, both in San Jose del Cabo; seafood at Luis Bulnes' new Galleon restaurant, Cabo San Lucas.

Famous Saloons
Hussong's Cantina, Ensenada; Los Gordos Cantina, Punta Banda; Hotel Serenidad Bar, Mulegé; any of the Buena Vista fishing-resort bars; La Perla outdoor café, La Paz; Finisterra patio bar, Cabo San Lucas. Try Bohemia and Pacifico beers if available.

Sights on or near the Highway
Bullring by the Sea, Playa Tijuana (*corridas* on selected summer Sundays only); Rosarito Beach Hotel, Playa Rosarito; the blowhole (La Bufadora), Punta Banda; the boojum forest, Vizcaíno Desert (El Rosario to Punta Prieta); all of Bahía de Los Angeles (especially Papa Diaz's chapel, made of solid Baja onyx); the plaza and mission at San Ignacio; the tropical river village of Mulegé; the Loreto mission; Carnaval at La Paz (Mardi Gras, held the week before Lent); El Triunfo, an old mining town; village of San Jose del Cabo; the harbor and Finisterra Hotel, Cabo San Lucas; ancient Indian cave paintings, many locations; the many half-moon-bay trailer parks on Concepción Bay.

Licenses, Permits
As of this writing, an immigration office has reopened on the highway about 15 miles south of Ensenada. The officers there check southbound vehicles for drunk drivers, guns, open containers and drugs. In the past year, driving while intoxicated has become a very serious offense in Baja and, as always, it invalidates your insurance if you have an accident. All members of your party will need tourist permits to proceed south, issuable at no cost on the spot, but all will need passports or birth certificates as proof of nationality.

You may travel anywhere in Mexico for up to 90 days on this permit, but if you choose to go on to mainland Mexico (there is a ferry from La Paz to Mazatlán and Acapulco), you will need special permits for all your vehicles. You can get these by presenting the proper registration for each vehicle at the Border Immigration Office. The ferry, by the way, is booked up six weeks in advance during the winter, so make reservations before leaving home if you plan to use it.

If you are trailering or carrying a car-top boat, you will need a boat permit. You sometimes can get your boat permit and Mexican fishing license when you buy vehicle insurance. Be sure to have with you both boat and trailer registration certificates. It is necessary for everyone on board the boat to have a fishing license, also. They are available for a week, a month or a year. Get boat permits and fishing licenses at the Mexico Office of Fisheries, 1010 Second Avenue, Room 1605, San Diego, California 92101; (619) 233-6956.

Pet Regulations
If you want to take your pet with you to Baja, you can, but first you must obtain an International Health Certificate from your veterinarian and then get it stamped by the Los Angeles office of the Mexican Consulate—before crossing the border. This costs $15.50 per pet. It can be done in person or by mail, but they accept only money orders, not personal checks. Call the Mexican Consulate at (213) 624-3261 for further information.

Complaint Department
If you have any legal problems or complaints while you are in Baja, the place to start resolving them is the Office for the Protection of Tourists,

with locations in Tijuana, Ensenada and La Paz. I have seen them really go to bat for tourists in squabbles involving overcharging, rip-offs and outright robberies.

Fishing

It is considered a heinous crime to come to Baja without going fishing. This is one of the world's leading game-fishing areas. There is a large party-boat fleet in Ensenada, and smaller boats are available at all locations mentioned here. Aluminum boats, 15 feet and up, are ideal, but do not bring a boat designed for lake or river fishing. Baja seas can kick up in a fury.

Best Trailer Park in Baja

Posada Concepción, Bahía Tordillo, 14 miles south of Mulegé.

Return to Espíritu

A deserted Baja island challenges 10 hardy adventurers

Emil Barjak

In 1983, as I was rafting the entire length of Mexico's Sea of Cortez with my Adventurers Club companions, the island of Espíritu Santo especially attracted my attention—turquoise waters, small romantic bays and clean, untouched beaches. I expressed then the idea to live at least one week on this wonderful spot . . . to fish and dive for our daily meals. Three years later, the dream was realized.

PHOTO: EMIL BARJAK

The island camp was hastily set up and then deserted by the anxious fishermen.

The members of our adventurous group included Dr. Ken Senter, our expedition surgeon from Los Angeles; George Andreos, who has explored California's Sierra Nevada with me many times; my longtime travel companion Isgo Lepejian; my brother-in-law, Raul Bulhosen, and my two nephews, Bernardo and Raul Jr., all from Mexico City; Baja fan and master fisherman Ron Nichols; and my son, Eduardo.

The adventure began in La Paz, on the gulf coast of Mexico's Baja peninsula, after a family vacation and reunion in Mexico City.

It had been a long haul for all the members of my family, as we arrived in Mexico City in our Winnebago. We had traveled from our home in Solana Beach, California, through Arizona, New Mexico and western Texas, entering Mexico from Laredo.

The roads in the United States and Mexico had been first class and always interesting, but living and traveling together for a longer amount of time—even in our spacious motorhome—proved to be strenuous for our spirits and bodies.

PHOTO: EMIL BARJAK

George, Ron, and the three boys return to Espiritu at sunset after an afternoon of diving and fishing.

Top, ***Eduardo and Raul Jr. check out the lava fields at Ceborneo en route to Mazatlan for the ferry trip to Baja.*** **Center,** ***Over his seasickness, George (left) shares a toast to health and friendship with Ron as they beat the heat and mosquitoes.*** **Bottom,** ***Eduardo's catch of the day, a snook, makes a fine dinner.***

PHOTOS: EMIL BARJAK

We arrived in Mexico's capital, and the driving of a large motorhome in this lively city with the most incredible traffic was an adventure in itself. Years ago, I had learned never to look in my rearview mirror while driving in Mexico City.

After we paid our dues by visiting most of my wife's family members, Eduardo, my nephews and I left in the motorhome for the long drive to Mazatlán on the Pacific coast. It was a diverse and inspiring trip, taking us from the central highlands to the lush and tropical coast, through big cities like Guadalajara and small villages.

Most of the time our meals were taken in little roadside restaurants where $1 (U.S.) would buy a dish of rice and chicken. Fruit stands along the way provided all kinds of exotic snacks, from mangoes to papayas to coconuts and pineapples. After two days traveling, we arrived in Mazatlán, where there was all the seafood one could imagine.

But as we drove into the harbor facilities to purchase the tickets for the ferry to La Paz, the long line of people waiting was not an optimistic sight to see. I heard some families had been waiting for three days. Getting the motorhome on the ship was hopeless, so I had to find a parking spot for it in Mazatlán, then find a truck with a passage ticket to ship our gear, including the inflatable raft and 25-horsepower motor, to La Paz on the Baja peninsula. My friends from California and brother-in-law Raul were waiting there. Luckily for us, there was an opportunity for a truck driver to add our gear to his load on his colorful truck, and a visit to the manager of the ferry secured us the passage.

As they say south of the border: *"Mexico magico!"* Everything is possible in this country.

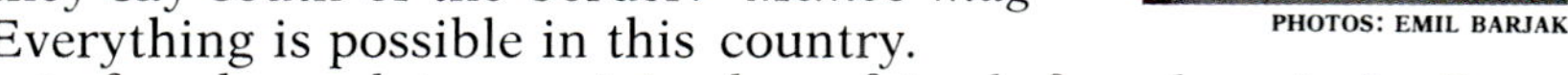

Twenty-four hours later, we joined our friends for a beer in La Paz.

For many years, I had been buying the food for our trips and planning the rations per person. But living on a tropical island would be different: no refrigeration, very little shade, night-and-day heat and humidity, and sand. We had to rely on our skill in fishing; no meat was necessary. Bread would go stale in two days, so potatoes were added for carbohydrates. Some noodles, cooking oil, rice, canned beans and oriental Top Ramen made up the rest; lots of beer, a half-ton of limes, and we were well equipped.

Our friend and local fisherman, Guadalupe, from La Paz, helped us with his dugout boat to load the gear and food for the crossing to the island. I had my inflatable Avon finely tuned.

Excitement, camaraderie, the unknown ahead of us, excellent fishing and diving—all these describe our anticipation in a situation like this.

We were just one or two miles out of La Paz when Ron locked the first fish, but he released the big bonita. We still had hours to travel. Three hours and 33 miles later, we entered a turquoise bay on the island of Espíritu Santo. It looked great; there was a mile-long beach, some mangroves, mountains in the background, and it was ours for a week.

With everybody's help, we had tents and mosquito screen up in no time. The flag of The Adventurers Club of Los Angeles was flying high on a fishing rod. We had a corner for beer and tequila, and Ken was named manager of the alcohol-and-lime department. The kitchen was set up in a rather quick and messy way. Everyone wanted to get in some fishing or snorkeling.

It must have been close to 5 P.M. when the first man complained about the number of mosquitoes. By 5:30, we were all jumping, clapping, hitting our faces and running for cover, but there was no place to hide. The mosquitoes, ants and fleas were eating us alive. Even taking a shower with repellent wouldn't help: the perspiration washed the Mus-kol away. Finally, we all joined George, who was sitting in the water with his beer and a lime in his hand.

Our romantic outing on a deserted island was agreeable again, and we sat in the shallow bay water until 8:30 P.M., when the long-expected breeze came up.

"Tomorrow we hit *dorados* (dolphin fish or mahi-mahi)," Ron kept dreaming.

"I'll supply lobster for everybody," my son, Eduardo, replied. There was peace and great friendship and warm beer for everybody on our island. By 9:30 the comfortable breeze had become a strong wind, and by 10 P.M., we had a full-size storm. We ran again for cover, this time from the sand and to save our supplies from blowing into the ocean. It was a disaster all over again, and one we had not expected in a romantic week on a deserted island. Yes, we were far away from stress, from traffic, from long office hours, credit cards and shopping, but we had traded them for 100°F-temperatures day and night, nonstop mosquitoes and other critters, a sandstorm, no fresh water to wash with, and three meals of fish a day. But no one asked to turn back or to move into a tourist hotel in La Paz. We were there to stay, for one week at least. Then, we'd return to Mazatlán for the motorhome journey home to California.

Every day there was some unexpected excitement. One evening a full-size highly poisonous scorpion came out of Raul's sleeping bag. Ken had to do some minor surgery on Ron's foot (with a Swiss Army pocketknife). George got deadly seasick in some 7- to 8-foot waves.

But we caught fish three times a day, all sizes and colors. We were diving and swimming into the night. And we heard some big lies about even bigger fish around the campfire as we enjoyed our warm beer.

The week was going by too fast, we agreed, as we packed our sandy gear. A big storm—a *chubasco*—was moving in. We had about three to four hours to make it back to La Paz, as the wind picked up again.

Then we were once again in the open sea, battling a tropical storm in a small inflatable raft. Our friend, George, did not have enough time to get seasick; the waves were too high, the clouds too dark and the lightning too close.

In all my years of traveling—to the source of the Nile River in Africa, to the headwaters of the Amazon, rafting the Sea of Cortez, sleeping in the treetops of the Central American jungle or reaching the 18,500-foot summit of Mexico's Pico de Orizaba—the words of James Carnegie, Earl of Southesk, come always to my mind.

"This open-air life suits me well, though when one considers it bit by bit, it does not seem so very charming. Long wearisome walks, indifferent monotonous eating, no sport to speak of, hard bed upon the ground, hot sun, wet; nevertheless, I am happier than I have been for years."

Counties Cork and Kerry

There's more than blarney to the southwest of Ireland

Michael Verdon

PHOTO: MICHAEL VERDON

A small child peers over the wall of the family home in County Kerry.

On a map, the southwest corner of Ireland looks like an angry fist. Four rugged, stumpy peninsulas jut into the churning Atlantic, with thin roads coursing through them like withered veins. Mountains, tall and spiked, give the appearance of tough, bumpy skin.

The angry coast seems also to express itself in its sports, or so I thought, sitting in my rented motorhome one day last summer, watching a group of Kerrymen play Gaelic football. In a brutal cross between soccer and rugby, the players chased after an oblong leather ball (slightly larger than an American football), bashing, kicking and mauling one another in the process. To this spectator, the final score appeared to be four bloody noses to three broken teeth.

The violent nature of Ireland's sporting activities, however, is in sharp contrast to the warmth and friendliness of her people.

During a two-week tour of counties Cork and Kerry, the closed fist of Ireland soon revealed itself as an open, beckoning palm, the extended fingers inviting me to explore its beautiful coastline.

For several reasons, early summer is the ideal time to visit Ireland. The weather is usually on good behavior (only three days of rain during

PHOTO: MICHELE BURGESS

A lone cottage looks out to sea on the Beara Peninsula in County Kerry.

Formerly an important port of call for trans-Atlantic ships, Cobh (the cove) of County Cork was the Titanic's *last port before sailing to disaster and the last sight of Ireland for thousands of Irish emigrants.*

my 14-day visit), and the hordes of tourists traveling in rented cars and buses don't begin to arrive until midsummer, so the hilly roads are virtually traffic-free.

PHOTO: MICHAEL VERDON

Motorhome rentals are available, and a list of approved companies can be obtained from the Irish Tourist Board at 757 Third Avenue, New York, New York 10017; (212) 418-0800. One of Ireland's leading rental companies, Dan Dooley Rent-a-Car, accepts bookings through its New Jersey office. For rental information, contact the company at P.O Box 340, Colonia, New Jersey 07067; (201) 381-8948.

I rented my motorhome in Cork, the republic's second-largest city, and quickly learned the rules of the road. First, traffic runs on the left side of the road, so you have to remember to watch for oncoming vehicles when making a right-hand turn. Once you become accustomed to the driver's position being on the right-hand side of the vehicle and learn to negotiate the narrow country roads, driving in Ireland is easy.

Having left the motorhome in the campground outside the city limits, I wandered around the hilly streets of Cork. When I went into shops, I was greeted with friendly questions because of my Yankee accent: Where was I from, how long was I staying, what did I think of Ireland, etc. I was also given dozens of suggestions on places to see, roads to take and restaurants to try.

The city of Cork was founded by St. Finbar in the late sixth century on dry land—actually an island—above the Great Marsh of Munster. All of the main thoroughfares of Cork were once waterways used by ships to load and unload cargo. The medieval city grew beyond its original walls, spreading uphill above the marsh and to the surrounding islands. By the eighteenth and nineteenth centuries, the old waterways were roofed over; today you cannot enter the city of Cork without crossing a bridge.

Little is left of medieval Cork, but you will notice how streets and waterways still intertwine in this city of bridges. Three outstanding bridges are St. Patrick's Bridge, leading from Patrick Street east to Waterford; the elegant Parliament Bridge, spanning the River Lee; and the South Gate Bridge, located at the south gate of the medieval walled city, which offers a view of the seventeenth-century ruins of Elizabeth Fort. Nearby, at the original site of Finbar's monastery, stands St. Finbar's Gothic cathedral, named for the city's patron saint and completed in 1870. The Red Abbey, a tall, gray limestone tower, is all that remains of the house of the Augustinian friars, founded around 1300.

Use of local red sandstone and gray limestone checkerboard patterns in more recent buildings is unique to Cork. Ornamental ironwork and elegant fanlights are some of the finishing touches.

Follow the signposted Tourist Trail for a great introduction to the city's important sites.

Five miles northwest of Cork lies the village of Blarney, home of the most visited castle in Ireland. The magnificent 84½-foot-high Blarney Castle was built with 12-foot-thick walls in 1446 by Cormac MacCarthy, Lord of Muskerry.

According to one of many local legends associated with the castle, a bygone member of the MacCarthy clan, who was born with a speech impediment, saved a young woman from drowning in a dangerous

PHOTO: MICHELE BURGESS

In the village of Annascaul, a local pub touts the favorite Irish stout.

stream. The woman turned out to be a witch and rewarded MacCarthy with one wish. He wished to speak properly, and the woman instructed him to go to the parapet of the castle and locate a certain stone, which would cure his impediment when he kissed it.

The castle's famous Blarney Stone draws thousands of visitors each year, who come hoping to acquire the gift of eloquence after kissing the stone. However, the stone is not easily accessible. One must hang head downward over the battlements on the south side of the castle.

From the area of Cork, I headed out into the open countryside. For 16 miles the road ran south, the sparkling ocean dropping in and out of sight on my left. I quickly learned how long it can take to travel a mile in Ireland because the roads—even the major ones—are hilly and winding, rising and falling like a series of crooked camel humps.

Kinsale, a picturesque little fishing harbor full of boats, eventually appeared. I drove slowly through the small village of winding streets lined by Georgian houses and was delighted to see a number of seafood restaurants clustered together. I later discovered that Kinsale is considered the gourmet capital of Ireland. I certainly had an unforgettable meal there in a restaurant called The Vintage.

The village of Kinsale played an important role in Irish history. Early invaders found it geographically desirable because it looked out across the sea to the mainland of Europe; its view is best appreciated from atop Compass Hill. Although an attempt to colonize the area with English settlers under Sir Walter Raleigh failed in the sixteenth century, Spanish troops landed at Kinsale in 1601 to help the Irish in a revolt that proved unsuccessful against the English. The defeat at Kinsale marked the end of Irish independence. A small museum in the restored Tholsel of 1706 contains relics of the siege of 1601 and other items of local interest.

On the south bank of the Bandon River, you'll view the ruins of Ringrone Castle; below stands Charles Fort, erected in 1677. Guarding the mouth of the harbor, the fort held off invading armies for centuries. Today's visitor can see how new walls were constructed with each new age—from the original stone walls to World War II concrete bunkers. As I drove the motorhome away from the massive walls, I felt dwarfed by the ancient history of Charles Fort, as well as the nearby Old Fort.

Just 10 miles south of Kinsale is the Old Head of Kinsale, a cliff overlooking the site where the *Lusitania* was torpedoed by a German submarine in 1915. The 265-foot-high promontory commands a fine coastal view.

In fact, history is everywhere along the coastline of County Cork—old ruins that vary from castles of Irish chieftains to the churches of invading Normans to the grassy remains of stone cottages from the nineteenth century.

From Kinsale, I passed through small villages—Timoleague, Clonakilty, Rosscarbery, Bantry—strung along the coast like beads on a necklace. All were much the same in appearance, with one main street lined on both sides by three-story houses, a few food stores and, invariably, seven or eight pubs. Pubs, by the way, play an important part in the Irish social scene and frequently offer excellent, economical meals.

At night, I usually stayed at one of the 20 campgrounds in County Cork. These are ideal because they are inexpensive, have shower facilities and are often scenic. A copy of *Caravan and Camping Parks*, available from the Irish Tourist Board, will help you plan your route. At times when I wanted to avoid other campers entirely, I stayed on empty stretches of bog, nothing stirring for miles around but the winds from the nearby sea.

The ancient city of Cork boasts three outstanding bridges and is laced with winding streets and waterways.

PHOTO: MICHAEL VERDON

After six days in County Cork and a portion of the County Kerry coastline, I reached Killarney, famed for its romantic countryside and the lakes of Killarney. Commercialized tourism has now surpassed the local industry of lacemaking here in Ireland's most popular tourist site.

In addition to the lakes region, recommended excursions outside of town include the ruins of Ross Castle, two miles southwest of Killarney, and Kate Kearney's Cottage, where a local beauty once dispensed "mountain dew" (poteen) to passing tourists around the turn of the nineteenth century. During the tourist season, vehicles must be left at the cottage before continuing to the Gap of Dunloe by foot, pony or horse-drawn jaunting car for a seven-mile-long track of spectacular mountain scenery. Jaunting cars are available for hire in Killarney with a guide who will take you where you want to go and tell you stories along the way.

After a brief stay in Killarney, I headed south toward Kenmare, the warm summer sun lighting up the brown bogs and valleys. That day was simply beautiful with the sunshine, the empty terrain and the blue ocean as backdrop. I felt somewhat like William Bulfin must have felt in 1905, when he wrote: "As you journey along the southern coast of Ireland, you cannot escape it. You derive pleasure from climbing the heath-clad mountains or roaming the beautiful valleys, or sweeping full speed over the slopes of the fertile hills." It's good to know that things haven't changed much in 80 years.

Of course, there are the dog days. In fact, only a few days later, southwesterly gales nearly overturned the motorhome just after rounding the famous Ring of Kerry, the 100-mile loop around the Iveragh Peninsula that begins and ends in Killarney. I drove along the coast that day, shaking, bumping and rattling against the head wind. I regretted having opted to take the scenic coastal route instead of following the main road.

Five miles later, as I crawled up the steepest slope that has ever been called a road, I was certain that the transmission would give out. But when I finally reached the crest of the hill, I was gratified by a view of Portmagee, a small port a few miles below, its whitewashed houses shining like pearls in the bright sunshine.

A few days later, I discovered what must be the most beautiful spot in Ireland: the Dingle Peninsula. It's out of the way, off the beaten track, but well worth the drive. The coastline road was breathtaking. To the left, across the sparkling inlet of blue water, four ranges of purplish mountains rose and fell like an irregular saw. Sea gulls hovered in the air, pivoting like ballerinas, screeching, then suddenly diving straight into the ocean, emerging with small fish in their beaks.

The Dingle Peninsula stretches out to sea for more than 30 miles, and the contrasts in scenery—from bogs to cliffs to mountains—make each mile unique. The town of Dingle is a small sleepy port, with fishing boats moored along the docks, nets and rowboats drying in the sun, and fishermen gathered in loose groups, speaking of the day's catch. Ten miles farther west, houses become scarce. The inhabitants speak Irish (Gaelic) as their native tongue; crossroads pubs and food shops are the only markers of civilization.

As I have said, I found the Irish to be an incredibly friendly people, but no one was as friendly as the old woman I met during my last few days in Dingle. On the day before I left the area, I was standing beside my motorhome, which was parked beside a stone wall. Except for a cottage some ways down the road, the land was empty, almost desolate. Patches of peat—the most common form of fuel for heating in rural Ireland—were neatly stacked in piles, and a slight breeze was rustling the thorn bushes along the lane. As I stood there, reflecting upon how lonely and beautiful the landscape was, I heard a voice calling me from the cottage.

I turned to find an old woman sauntering toward me. She was wearing a thick black dress and her shoulders were draped in an ancient gray shawl. She repeated whatever she had said, but I still couldn't make it out. Then it dawned on me, she was speaking Irish.

When she came closer, she realized that I was not a fellow countryman.

"And where might you be coming from?" she asked in English.

"Dingle," I replied.

Her eyes lit up. "You're no Galway man, sure."

"No, I'm American."

"American, is it?" she asked. "I have a niece in America. In Chicago. Maire Sograno's her name now."

Eventually the woman invited me in for a cup of tea. She led me into the cottage and pointed to a wooden bench where I was to sit while she prepared the tea. The room was clean and bare, but comfortable. The peat fire glowing in the hearth gave it a safe, snug feeling. On a table beside the stone wall stood a statue of St. Jude, and beside that were several yellowing photos.

Returning with the tea, my hostess commenced to tell me about the people in the photographs—two sons and a deceased husband. The sons wanted her to come and live with them in Dublin, but she refused. "This is my home," she insisted. "I was born in this area and, please God, I will die here."

She went on and on, telling me how harsh the winter had been, how the small farmers of the area had suffered because of it, how her wee vegetable patch was in tatters, how quickly Ireland was changing. While listening to her, I felt touched—touched because even a lifetime of hardship had not embittered her. On the contrary, still active at the age of 77, she took pride in her home and her family. And it was touching because she had invited me—a total stranger—into her home to tell me of herself and her loved ones.

This was typical of what I experienced many times in Ireland, selfless hosts who made me feel comfortable without expecting anything in return. The Irish have a saying for it: *Céad Míle Fáilte*—"a hundred thousand welcomes."

Combined with the wonderful scenery and historical attractions, *Céad Míle Fáilte* will one day lure me back to the friendly Emerald Isle.

Special Features

Dollar and Sense

Travelers have a choice of several convenient resources for obtaining cash and services on the road

Dick Gould

It may have been the development of the modern recreational vehicle that opened the nation's roads to a casual kind of travel our grandparents wouldn't have imagined. But it is the banking business of the '80s that provides the services that free us to wander in our RVs anywhere our whims may lead us for a week, a month, a year, or perhaps even longer.

We don't have to carry everything along with us, not even all of the cash we'll need, as Grandma and Grandpa did. However, we have to plan carefully for access to enough money to provide all our needs while we're away.

And, though there are many who live full time in their wheeled estate, few ever travel so lightly, so far, or so long as to not leave something, somewhere, to which to return sometime. So arrangements must be made for someone (a relative, friend, or perhaps a bank) to care for those things in the rightful owner's absence.

The key to this life-style is choosing which banking services to use, when to use them and under what circumstances. Credit cards, money orders, several different kinds of checks and vouchers, a bank's trust department, or maybe just a reliable friend back home—each is effective in certain situations.

All are generally dependable—except perhaps in those occasional dire moments when they are most needed! Local money changers can balk at the simplest of suspicions, and sometimes for no apparent reason at all! That's why it's best not to rely too heavily on only one or two money-changing methods.

Such crashes in confidence are related usually to the traveling stranger's inability to identify himself to the satisfaction of the local businessman, or occasionally to his inability to convince the local people that he is indeed "good for it."

"We recommend that anyone who expects to travel where he or she is not known should carry at least two kinds of reliable identification," advises Ann Betts, an assistant cashier at First Virginia Bank. "A driver's license is usually acceptable," she adds, "or something of the kind, with your picture on it."

Ironically, the stumbling block that trips many longtime or full-time RVers is the accumulation of several forms of identification, each of them generally acceptable, but showing different addresses.

It is possible, for example, that a full-time RVer could have a driver's license from Pennsylvania, a major credit card listing an address in Iowa and a vehicle registered in California. Should a banker or businessman be blamed for hesitating to pay out cash on the basis of such identification?

Some full-time RVers seem to resent the need to return to a specific place at a certain time at least once a year in order to maintain a driver's license, vehicle registration, a book of personal checks and a major credit card, all showing the same "permanent legal address." It's not such a big deal.

It's no problem to have the RV inspected and the tags renewed in Virginia while we're back home for Christmas. While I'm at it, I can pay the annual rental on the post office box, stop at the bank to renew acquaintances—and then we're ready to take off again whenever we want.

If we want to stay away for another year, our son can stop by the house every few days to make sure everything is kosher, an automatic answering machine on the telephone will record incoming calls to which I can listen from any other phone in the world, and the postman will deliver our mail to the house, put it in the post office box or forward it, as instructed.

Another convenient option for receiving mail while on the road is the Good Sam Club's Mail Forwarding Service. Members pay for this in advance by calendar quarter. Club headquarters is used as their mailing address, and headquarters forwards mail to whatever en-route addresses members provide while traveling. A telephone-message service is also available to Good Sammers who are long-term travelers.

Generally, for us it has been most practical to have the mail accumulate in the post office box until my son picks it up. He can look through it before our next regular telephone chat, tell me about anything that needs my prompt attention, and follow through with any errands that should be done immediately.

RVers who have no close relative, no dependable neighbor, no good friend on whom they can rely, might consult an attorney or the trust department of their bank, either of whom may be willing (for a fee) to pay certain bills automatically when they're due.

Even without such a trust agreement, officials of several different banks advised me to retain a regular and cordial business relationship with a large, full-service commercial bank, preferably one with direct

Automatic Teller Machines

Sherry McBride

The ATM card issued by First Interstate Bank is useful nationwide and even in Canada through the Cirrus network.

The newest form of cash access is the ATM (Automatic Teller Machine) card, offered by most banks, each with its own peculiar characteristics. Bank of America's Versatel Card is utilized for a variety of services, from depositing or transferring funds to making credit-card payments and obtaining cash. The most important thing to note is that the ATM card is the equivalent of a personal check. Whatever you withdraw comes directly out of your checking account. There is no interest and no charge for the service, but if you don't keep careful records, you could run out of funds faster than you realize.

In order to obtain national or even international use of your ATM card, you'll want one that is issued by an institution, bank or savings and loan that is a member of an extended banking network. Bank of America is a member of the Plus system. Other banks in this system include Chase Manhattan and Valley Bank of Nevada. The B of A Versatel Card holder can walk into any of approximately 2,000 banks and savings and loans throughout the United States and Canada to obtain cash. There is a transaction charge of $1, and you're only able to withdraw cash. The other banking services are not available through any institution except your originating bank.

To find out where your ATM card can be used, request a directory from the institution issuing the card. These are available free of charge. If you can't get a directory at your local bank, ask for the toll-free phone number to call from wherever you happen to be, so you can find out immediately where your card will be honored. Obviously, it's wiser to know in advance.

There are places, of course, where your ATM card won't be welcome. The majority of the institutions participating in the extended banking systems are in major cities. You should be aware of this fact and plan accordingly. In other words, try not to get caught without a nickel in Podunk.

In addition to the Plus system, there are other networks used by some banks and savings and loans, such as Cirrus, which is used by First Interstate and City banks.

While all of this is intended to provide basic information about one of the banking options available to today's travelers, our suggestion is that you discuss your travel plans with your home bank representative before making any decisions. Find out what is offered there, then shop around and compare, as you would for a new RV. It will be worth the time and effort involved to be sure you've laid a sound foundation for keeping your cash flowing as smoothly as your wheels are rolling wherever you go.

connections to the Federal Reserve System's data network and preferably located in the same community where I maintain a permanent legal address.

Before leaving on any extended trip, several bankers advised, be sure to sign and file an electronic fund-transfer agreement with that bank. These agreements vary slightly from bank to bank but, in general, they authorize the transfer of specified amounts of money on the basis of a telephone call. Many such agreements include a password system, so the bank staff can verify the voice on the phone.

The bankers all agreed that with such an agreement on file at the home bank and suitable identification offered by the motorhomer electronic transfers are the easiest, quickest and most reliable method. They're also expensive. Fees vary, but expect to pay from $10 to $25 per transfer, regardless of the amount sent.

Most banks offer some kind of access to networks of automatic teller machines (ATM). See page 000 for information about this newest banking option.

Traveler's checks remain one of the safest means of carrying money. They are available free at Bank of America (although other institutions may charge), they are good for an indefinite period and they are accepted almost anywhere in the world. There are a couple of problems with using them, however. Sometimes, you may need to pay for $20 worth of gas or groceries with a $100 traveler's check, and the proprietor may not be able to cash it for you. Also, if you run out of traveler's checks, you'll need cash to buy more.

The plastic-money system is so easy, it's difficult to imagine doing business without a credit card. No one card is accepted everywhere, so the wise traveler will choose more than one of the major cards, such as VISA, MasterCard, American Express or the new Sears' Discover Card. Those issued by small savings and loans and hometown banks seldom are accepted all over the nation. Credit cards allow you to obtain cash advances at any bank that accepts that particular card, a true convenience when you need anywhere from $10 to $100 while on the road. And if you are careful to pay the outstanding balance before the next thirty-day payment is due, you won't have to pay the interest charges.

Chain-store cards are useless except for purchases within the issuing chain. Gas station cards can be convenient, but read the fine print to be sure they offer terms that fit the circumstances.

A better deal may be postal money orders or Series-E government bonds. Postal money orders can be bought in any amount up to $700, the fees are minimal, and they don't have to be mailed. You can carry them with you. There's a wait of six months after purchase before Series-E bonds can be cashed, but if you plan to buy them in advance, they can be cashed easily, they offer much the same sort of safety as traveler's checks and, instead of charging a fee, they pay interest.

But when all is said and done, never sneer at the serviceability of the much-maligned personal check. A lot of businesspeople who say they don't accept personal checks will in fact cash one now and then—especially in an emergency.

Flea for All

Buy, sell and swap your way across the country through an endless procession of flea markets and swap meets

Barbara Leonard

Wanted: *Old U.S. Route 66 sign, posters of Jean Harlow, crocheted pillows, unpolished fire agate, porcelain dolls, Elvis memorabilia, Log Cabin Syrup tins, silk flowers, pewter spoons, Bavarian cuckoo clocks, and linen handkerchiefs.*

That's an unusual assortment of articles, true, but not an uncommon one, found in hundreds of classified advertisements across the country as "fleas" and "swappers" multiply.

Flea markets are attracting people of all ages, from every background and every corner, but perhaps best suited to this mobile, fun and often lucrative life-style are RVers, especially retirees who want to supplement fixed funds.

With your natural penchant for travel and socializing, and with a little research and some careful planning, you too may discover that flea marketing could be your ticket to spending more time on the road.

PHOTO: BARBARA LEONARD

Personalized horseshoes are among the many specialty items available at flea markets.

What Is a Flea?

Maybe it started in 1626 when Peter Minuit, the governor of the Dutch West India Company, bought Manhattan Island from the Indians for $24 worth of beads and trinkets. Whatever the origin, bartering is big business today. Whether done for goods, money, services or talent, selling and swapping are no longer merely hobbies or the part-time fundraisers they once were; they have reached the status of a legitimate occupation. Entrepreneurs are found behind tables at garage sales, flea markets, swap meets, festivals, fairs, mall shows, rummage sales, farmers' markets, carnivals, antique shows, RV shows and club rallies. Al-

PHOTOS: BARBARA LEONARD

Top, *A wide array of gems and rocks is displayed for two weeks every January and February in Quartzsite, Arizona.* Bottom, *Tony Langdorf of Pueblo, Colorado, the owner of Artco Creations, a glass-blowing concession, designs and produces original works.*

though there was once a well-defined difference—swap meets were relegated to secondhand items, and flea markets specialized in handmade arts and crafts—most lines have been crossed today. However, a few pure flea markets remain, such as the rock and gem shows, where only true artisans abound.

How to Get Started

"Find your forte," urges Dan Moss of Berkeley, California, "and pursue it." Moss, who floundered for more than a year between antique furniture and tools, finally found his calling with postcards, baseball cards and Beatles paraphernalia.

If you are a shopper, your job is simple: Read the Yellow Pages and the classifieds, then follow the signs to more than 3,000 assorted markets annually, and seek out the best bargains.

If, however, you are a swapper—or would like to be—some careful thought and planning are necessary. How far are you willing to travel? How much money do you need or want to make? Are you 70 years old or older, so your annual earned income has no bearing on your Social Security pension? Is this going to be a weekend job or a lifetime career?

There are dozens of other factors to consider before you start flea-ing. Some of the most important are: careful examination of your special interests; a close look at any talents that might be salable; and, if you are half of a couple, ascertaining if your companion shares your desire to enter the world of flea markets.

Then look around you. Is every nook and cranny filled with antiques, collectibles, clothing or junk? Do you have a garage, attic or basement

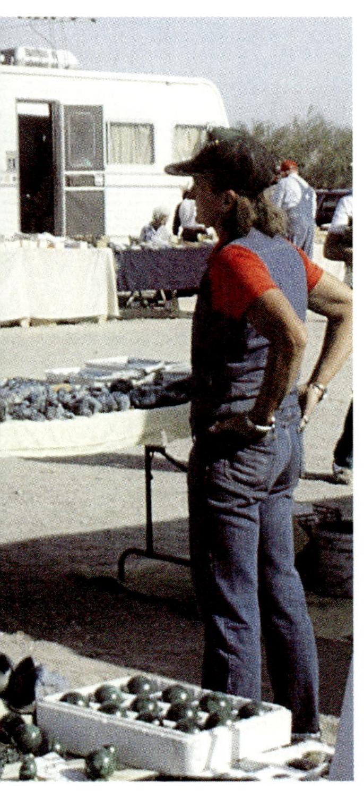

bursting with nineteenth-century mason jars, old books or great-granddad's garden tools? Can you bear to part with them? If so, then secondhand stuff may be your niche. Once you have decided on a particular item or items, learn everything you can about them. Study the market, attend as many shows as possible and ask questions of vendors with similar goods. Familiarize yourself with the history, materials and value of your wares, so you know what to buy when it's time to replenish your supply and what to charge your customers. Brush up on geography. In other words, know your subject matter and your market. The residents of Mobile, Alabama, are unlikely candidates for your used ski gear.

Many RVers choose to go into retail sales and find it very rewarding. Harold and Kathyrine Raysor of Pennsylvania sell a full line of knives, including their most popular item, the Survival Knife.

Select relatively small, compact and easy-to-transport items such as cameras, purses or jewelry, and buy from a wholesaler, a mail-order company or a source outside of the country. Bob Burns of Phoenix, Arizona, shops across the border in Mexico for leather goods—belts, handbags, jackets. With the excellent rate of exchange and the generally lower prices, he's able to double and often triple his investment. Buying 35mm cameras through a mail-order firm for $5.80 each in bulk orders turns quite a profit for Bill Williams at the Pasadena Rose Bowl Flea Market, where he often gets as much as seven times his outlay.

It is this kind of shopping that makes RVing and flea-ing such a perfect combination. RVers have a mobile stockroom, a roving warehouse that they can fill with indigenous goods from one state or region and transport to another. This is a definite edge over the less-mobile populus. On your visit to New Jersey, did you notice the lack of silver and turquoise jewelry? Why not fill that gap the next time you visit New Mexico? And how about that thick, rich, natural maple syrup from Maine? Wouldn't that be a big seller in Montana? It is this kind of planning that can make flea marketing a pay-as-you-go proposition.

Creative and clever RVers will have no trouble taking their show on the road. Remember, what comes naturally to you may be impossible for others. "I never dreamed that face-painting would go over so big," said Joan Molino of Bell, California. "Of course, you have to concentrate more on festivals and fairs to get the younger audience, but what fun!"

Do you sew, crochet, knit, do macramé or paint? Can you carve wood, work with silver, metal or glass? How about that mouth-watering recipe of Aunt Martha's for apple fritters? You could duplicate it in small quantities in the privacy of your RV galley, or you might think big and rent/buy a mobile kitchen concession. Have neighbors complimented you on your green thumb, admiring a spring bouquet of flowers or your culinary skills, sampling your homemade jam? Do you have any photographic skills to capture market memories on film and sell them to vendors and customers alike?

Tony Langdorf is a glassblower from Pueblo, Colorado, who tried something a little different and met with immediate success. "I discovered how to sprinkle gold or silver particles into my long-stemmed flowers," says Langdorf, "and the result is a glimmering, eye-catching creation. I also designed my own koala bear and unicorn-head earrings. The teenage girls are crazy about them." Although he was doing a lively

Precious and semiprecious stones are offered in abundance from coast to coast.

PHOTOS: BARBARA LEONARD

business at Quartzsite, Arizona, when we interviewed him, the artist admitted that he prefers indoor accommodations for his line of work.

What Will It Cost?

The initial investment to become a roving entrepreneur can vary from a few dollars to a few thousand, depending on your specialty and where you sell. If you maintain your permanent home and drive to a weekend swap meet to sell apples grown in your backyard, your expenses will obviously be minimal: gas, parking fee (free to $5) and dealer fee ($2 to $10 per day). Figure on an additional $5 to $20 should you stay overnight and require full hookups. If, on the other hand, you have decided to do the rock-and-gem circuit from coast to coast, you will probably require a substantial investment, perhaps as much as $3,000 to cover materials (stones, machinery, lapidary tools, settings), display equipment (tables, chairs, awnings, cases), extensive travel expenses and higher rental fees at longer shows such as the Quartzsite, Arizona, Main Event ($135 to $183 per space for one to two weeks).

To become a participant in any circuit, you should join an appropriate organization (such as The All Rockhounds Pow Wow Club of America Incorporated, 7043 South Clement, Tacoma, Washington 98409) and subscribe to a related publication (see listings at end of article).

Loretta and Charles Hoye, formerly of Massachusetts, appear to have the gem circuit down to a science. "We currently live in New Mexico," explains Loretta, "where we really appreciate the scenery, weather and proximity to rock and mineral sites and shows." The Hoyes average 22 shows a year and manage to plan them to coincide with harvest time. "I can buy 200 pounds of carrots in Idaho for next to nothing, bushels of cherries in Montana, and make it home in time to can them so we have this produce all winter," boasts Loretta. "Why, we could sell canned goods," says Charles, "if we weren't already so busy with stones and jewels."

When and Where

Just as snowbirds follow the sun, dedicated shoppers and swappers must be prepared to follow their calling. Careful planning, both seasonal and weekly, is a necessity. Is there a midweek market you must attend to replenish your wares and a Sunday show that you want to do? What is the distance between them? Are you taking weather and road conditions into consideration? Should you have made reservations? Can you park your RV on the site, or do you need a campground?

If you live and sell in the Sun Belt, you've got a 12-month operation—if you want it. Generally, major flea markets in four-season states run

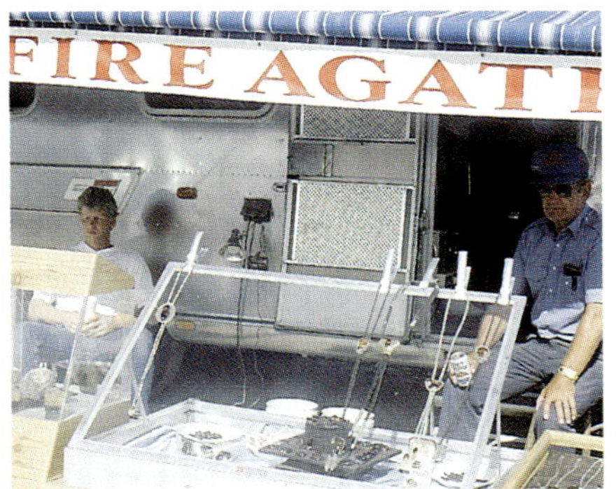

Left, *Food of all kinds is usually available at flea markets and swap meets.* Right, *Fire agate, both rough and polished, is Roy Barclay's specialty.*

from spring to fall. The exceptions to this in many areas are Christmas shows, which can be bonanzas for arts-and-crafts flea marketers. Your crocheted toaster cover or hand-carved pelican may make a very welcome stocking filler.

Seasonal food specialties are guaranteed best-sellers. Your secret family recipe for butter-rich fudge, wrapped in festive paper, could pay for your entire holiday gift list. We recently found intriguing elephant ears (a sweet Mexican concoction similar to *churros*), Indian tacos and delectable morsels of French-fried artichokes, broccoli and zucchini at the Main Event in Quartzsite. Food vendors at such events are indispens-

Major Markets

Although there may be as many as 5,000 flea markets and swap meets across the country, here are a few worthy of special mention due to their size or specialty.

• **Quartzsite, Arizona:** This small community of 300 may draw the largest number of RVs in the world over a two-week period in late January, early February. Located on Interstate 10, 22 miles east of Blythe, California, and 72 miles south of Lake Havasu City, Arizona, this desert happening features three enormous shows in one. The **Main Event Annual Gemboree** [(602) 927-5213], the **Quartzsite Pow Wow Gem and Mineral Show** [(602) 927-6325], and the **Tyson Wells Sell-A-Rama** [(602) 927-6364] attract an estimated 500,000 to 750,000 participants. Parking in private parks and on free public land is plentiful. • **Pasadena, California:** Featuring "everything under the sun," the **Rose Bowl Flea Market & Swap Meet** [(213) 588-4411] accommodates more than 1500 dealers and 50,000 shoppers. Open the second Sunday of every month, 9 A.M. to 3 P.M., the market is located on the Pasadena Rose Bowl grounds at Rosemont Avenue and Arroyo Boulevard.

• **Orlando, Florida:** Not far from Walt Disney World on U.S. Highway 17-92 north of Orlando, **Flea World** [(305) 645-1792] is the country's largest market located under one roof. Started in 1982, this tremendous undertaking comprises 104 acres, 1,700 booths, 3,000 parking spaces, a 100-person people-mover and 96 concessions. The market is open year-round on Fridays, Saturdays and Sundays from 8 A.M. to 5 P.M. • **Albuquerque, New Mexico:** The **Open Air Flea Market** [(505) 881-6228], situated on Central N.E. between Louisiana and San Pedro, is open year-round on Saturday and Sunday and draws between 600 and 800 dealers. • **New Hope, Pennsylvania:** A treasure chest of antiques, collectibles and arts and crafts are featured at the **Country Host Flea Market** [(215) 477-4541] from the last week of March to December, 8 A.M. to dusk. Located on U.S. Highway 202, one mile north of the Holiday Inn, it is open on Saturday, Sunday and holidays. • **Canton, Texas:** Located two blocks north of the courthouse, the **First Monday Trade Day** [(214) 567-4300] market attracts up to 2,000 dealers on the first Monday of each month and the preceding Friday, Saturday and Sunday. No animals are allowed.

Left, ***Colorful cut glass is displayed in an old wheelbarrow.*** **Right,** ***Bright wind socks are hung out to attract the passing customer.***

PHOTOS: BARBARA LEONARD

able, so if you fancy yourself behind a stove—although it's hard, hot work and requires a considerable investment—you may find yourself managing the most successful concession in the market.

How to Sell

We've all walked into a store at one time or another without intending to buy, when the irrepressible smile of the salesperson or the colorful display changed our minds. Attitude and arrangement are very important for successful sales. Even if you're selling junk, it can be attractively displayed in logical order. Once again, planning is the key. Make certain you have sufficient merchandise to display before setting up shop, but not so much that you can't handle it all securely; there are sticky fingers, even at flea markets.

Some sellers prefer to tag everything and keep the tags as the items are sold to determine their profit and inventory. Others keep a log. However you prefer to do it, you should keep accurate records for yourself and for the Internal Revenue Service, which may or may not contact you (profits are potentially taxable income). Many markets collect a certain percentage of sales to go into a general tax pot, whereas others ask for voluntary submissions at the end of the meet. It is best to determine the restrictions at the beginning of the show and abide by them.

You must also decide whether you are willing or able to accept personal checks or credit cards. Most weekenders deal only in cash (make certain you have plenty of change); participants at longer shows consider checks but, as in any other venture, get burned when they bounce.

Whether you decide to become a weekend shopper or a seasonal swapper, to sell candy apples or Captain Marvel comics, you are sure to enjoy the hopping about, the merry banter and the heartwarming camaraderie of the life-style, according to those who have already been bitten by the flea. Good luck!

Cinder Fever

Century-old narrow-gauge steam trains travel some of the Southwest's most scenic mountain terrain

C. J. Burkhart

PHOTO: C.J. BURKHART

All aboard for an unforgettable ride on a steam-engine train.

Now, just hold on a minute. There's no use calling your doctor, writing the American Medical Association, taking aspirin and drinking lots of liquids, conferring with your pharmacist, spraying disinfectants, or running for the hills. If you already have it, it's too late, and if you haven't caught it as yet, you undoubtedly will. And, once you have it, there is no known cure, so don't try to fight it.

There are only a few isolated places remaining where you can contract this "delightful" disease, and two of the most contagious areas are located in southern Colorado and northern New Mexico.

By now, you've guessed this exactly isn't a critical illness. Far from it. "Cinder fever" is a warm, nostalgic feeling that can be transmitted only by huge, clanking, hissing, smoking and lovable old steam locomotives.

Unfortunately for steam-engine devotees, the more efficient, but far less captivating diesel locomotives have mostly replaced these belching behemoths, and you'll be hard put to find many still puffing away in America. But if you diligently search, you can still discover a few.

Situated about 100 driving miles from each other are two of the country's most outstanding steam locomotives. One, the Cumbres & Toltec Scenic Railroad (C&TS), originates in either Chama, New Mexico, or Antonito, Colorado; the other, the Durango & Silverton Narrow Gauge Railroad (D&SNG), travels a spectacular route between Durango and Silverton, Colorado. Both are descendants of the historic Denver and

PHOTO: C.J. BURKHART

Snow still frosts the mountain tops into the summer in Colorado as the Durango & Silverton Narrow Gauge Railroad (D&SNG) travels a spectacular route between the two cities.

Rio Grande Railway Company (D&RG), which for decades operated trains throughout the Rockies.

Fortunately, you will find that motoring to the locations of these two premier narrow-gauge relics through picturesque landscape is easy. If you're in the Santa Fe, New Mexico, area, drive 106 miles northwest on U.S. Highway 84, turn north on State Route 17, and within a couple of miles you'll enter Chama, the C&TS line's southern terminus. To find the D&SNG Railroad, just continue northwest on U.S. Highway 84 to Pagosa Springs, Colorado, turn left on U.S. Highway 160, and 60 miles later you'll arrive in historic Durango, this branch's southernmost terminal.

On the way to Durango, an icy, clear Colorado lake tempts RV anglers to try and catch their dinner.

PHOTOS: C.J. BURKHART

Should you be RVing through Colorado, follow U.S. Highway 550, called the Million Dollar Highway, south to Durango, or head south on Interstate 25 to U.S. Highway 160. Follow it west to U.S. Highway 285 or U.S. Highway 84, where you turn south to reach Antonito or Chama.

To facilitate maneuvering through mountainous terrain, all the original Denver and Rio Grande railroad tracks were narrow-gauge type with rails 3 feet apart, instead of 4 feet 8½ inches, as are standard gauge. With the narrow gauge, construction was less expensive, as were the engines and cars.

During 1881, the D&RG began converting to standard gauge because narrow-gauge outfits could not interconnect with the ever-expanding standard lines. Due to declining business, D&RG's Silverton became the only remaining narrow-gauge train that showed a profit during the early 1960s.

By January 1951, the D&RG had ceased hauling passengers on the Cumbres route, and in 1967 the directors decided to abandon the Antonito-Durango-Farmington line. In an effort to preserve a section of this scenic route as a tourist attraction, interested individuals inaugurated a "Save-the-Cumbres" campaign. By July 1970, New Mexico and Colorado had established a Railroad Authority and, for $545,000, purchased the 64-mile-long section of track between Chama and Antonito. On July 26, 1971, Scenic Railway Incorporated of Los Altos, California, began transporting passengers on the "new" Cumbres & Toltec Scenic Railroad.

Because these fascinating railroad journeys are very popular, it's necessary to make advance reservations as early as possible, especially if you plan a summer trip. To obtain additional information on the Silverton trip, contact the Durango & Silverton Narrow Gauge Railroad Company at 479 Main Avenue, Durango, Colorado 81301; (303) 247-2733. Contact the Cumbres & Toltec Scenic Railroad at P.O. Box 789, Chama, New Mexico 87520; (505) 756-2151; or P.O. Box 668, Antonito, Colorado 81120; (303) 376-5483.

In 1879, the Denver & Rio Grande Railway founded the city of Durango and, due to the mining boom, completed the 45-mile-long Silverton spur in only 11 months. Considering the difficult territory that had to be conquered and the brutal winter weather, this was an amazing feat.

Top, ***In Silverton, the old Wells Fargo building is one of the sights to see during a $2\frac{1}{2}$-hour lunch stop before returning to Durango. One-way trips are also available.*** Bottom, ***The Silverton Mixed travels a scenic route through Animas Valley from Durango to Silverton, where passengers may debark for sightseeing.***

On May 23, 1981, the entire line was sold for than $2 million to the D&SNG railroad.

After D&SNG, directed by Charles E. Bradshaw, assumed ownership, numerous improvements were begun to improve engines, tracks and other work equipment. Later more trains were added to the schedule to accommodate the increasing number of passengers, and spectacular winter trips were instituted. Restoration of coach No. 350, The Alamosa, originally built in 1880, was also accomplished. Presently, No. 350 accompanies all trips as a nostalgic parlor car that, for a supplementary fare, offers deluxe service and seating, a bar and a delightfully different style in which to travel through the majestic Animas Valley.

This most unusual national historic landmark, which is only 3 feet wide but 240,000 feet long, follows the Animas River as it serpentines between the San Juan Mountains' lofty peaks. Although the Silverton travels only between Durango and Silverton, and "speeds" along like an overweight, over-the-hill snail, it is one of America's most prized trains. To accommodate more passengers, "double-headers" (two locomotives) have been added, but even so, seating space is quickly filled and advance reservations are almost always necessary.

For summer and autumn excursions, reserved seating fares (no unreserved seats are offered) range from $10.65 for children 5 through 11 years of age to $21.25 for adults at the time of this writing. Charges for the shorter, less expensive winter trips are $9 and $18, respectively, and many enthusiasts claim winter trips are more fun with more dramatic scenery. Not included in these costs, which are subject to change from year to year, are lunches and refreshments. And upon request, the railroad office will mail your tickets to you in advance of your departure.

Due to its slow pace and numerous stops, you may think the Silverton "Haphazard Express." However, it maintains a relatively rigid departure-and-arrival schedule. From mid-May to the end of October, trains leave the Durango station at 8:30 A.M., stop in Silverton for a $2\frac{1}{4}$-hour lunch break and arrive back in Durango at 5:10 P.M. One-way and inverse-direction trips are also available, but you'll need overnight accommodations in Durango or alternate transportation back to your original departure location. During the peak summer period, from June through August, a second train operates on a 9:30 A.M. to 6:10 P.M. schedule to accommodate the growing number of cinder-fever victims.

After lunching in Silverton, most passengers take a stroll through this small, picturesque and historic nineteenth-century town, where some of the West's wealthiest silver kings swiftly acquired immense fortunes and even more swiftly squandered them.

Plan to arrive at the D&SNG Durango depot a little early so, in addition to securing a good spot in the nearby parking lot, you can mingle with the expectant crowd, inspect the quietly hissing and grumbling locomotive, explore the old-time depot, and in general soak up some soot-and-cinders atmosphere.

Soon after settling into your seat, the train's wheels will commence their rhythmic clickity-clack, and you'll begin swaying to the car's easy rocking motion while your mind imperceptibly slips into the past. Close your eyes, just for a moment, and envision the car filled with nineteenth-century characters—crusty old prospectors, stone-faced gunmen, shifty-eyed gamblers, citified lawyers, demure ladies, rugged cattlemen, savory merchants, bankers and millionaires, each of whom adds a romantic aura to your legendary odyssey.

As you hustle along at a rollicking 15 miles an hour, you'll have time to relish the superb vistas in this remote, 2-million-acre wilderness that can only be explored on foot, by horseback or on D&SNG's train trips. In addition to the leisurely pace, numerous stops are made to refill the locomotive's water tank, to unload freight, pick up backpackers, fishermen and hikers, and to photograph both the train and the spectacular scenery.

During warm weather, roofed gondola cars provide passengers with a refreshing, open-air ride. It's a super way to get a brisk, unobstructed view of the valley and soaring peaks that squeeze in on both sides. Also, on summer and autumn trips, refreshment cars provide coffee, soft drinks and snacks; lunches and alcoholic beverages are added for winter jaunts.

Throughout the entire trip, you'll be treated to an outstanding parade of breathtaking scenery and historical attractions. Some of the most noteworthy include the 253-foot-long Animas River Bridge, Trimble Hot Springs, the strikingly scenic Highline in Animas Canyon, Needleton Stage Stop, Graystone and Garfield mountains, Cascade Canyon and the famous Champion Mine.

A pleasant, two-hour trip east of Durango offers another venue for trekking back into history and prolonging your enjoyment of cinder fever. Here at Chama, New Mexico, the Cumbres & Toltec Scenic Railroad offers a trip that in some respects is similar to the Durango and Silverton excursion, but in many ways is entirely different. Its 64 miles of track wriggle through northern New Mexico and southern Colorado's imposing San Juan Mountains, paralleling the Continental Divide for many miles and then crossing the 10,022-foot-high Cumbres and 10,230-foot-high La Manza passes.

When you hear two rolling, throaty blasts from the locomotive's whistle and the engine's husky "chuf, chuf," and see a tower of black smoke that would make a steam locomotive aficionado's heart skip a beat, you'll know your fascinating sojourn into yesteryear has begun. On either the New Mexico Express from Chama or the Colorado Limited out of Antonito, present schedules provide 6½-hour excursions Friday through Tuesday, from June through mid-October. Current fares range from $24 for adults to $9 for children 11 years old and under (fares are subject to change). Unpaid reservations are held until 45 minutes prior to departure, but prepaid reservations are guaranteed. All seating is on a reserved basis, so you should experience no difficulties.

The C&TS train also has open, unroofed gondola cars that may be used by all passengers. There are no seats in these cars so you must stand, but it's great fun to watch the scenery pass by from this sunny, open-air vantage point. Of course, there will be some cinders and smoke, but that's what it's all about.

While you savor the enchanting nineteenth-century ambiance, your train—looking somewhat like a toy as it animatedly huffs and puffs up steep grades and across vast, flower-strewn meadows—steadily climbs into the superb San Juan high country. As in a huge Cinemax extravaganza, broad, lush valleys; jagged peaks; cool, dusky forests; bubbling streams; and glistening lakes ease by. Rocky Windy Point, slender Cascade Trestle some 409 feet above Cascade Creek's deep chasm, Tanglefoot's nearly full-circle curve, dusky Toltec Tunnel, tight Whiplash Curve and cramped Calico Cut add their magic to an already fascinating spectacle.

At a former Colorado construction camp called Osier, located about halfway between Chama and Antonito, the Colorado Limited and the New Mexico Express meet. Here the trains stop and crews swap engines for return trips. While you wait, you can enjoy the beautiful scenery and eat a delicious buffet luncheon. Or, if you prefer, bring your own picnic basket stuffed with your favorite goodies. There is an indoor dining room but, if the weather permits, dine outdoors on picnic tables or on the colorfully flowered meadows.

Through-passengers must change trains at Osier and, as the railroad does not provide alternate return transportation, commuters must make their own arrangements or obtain passage on subsequently scheduled trains. This usually requires advance reservations.

By now you should have a thriving case of cinder fever and an urge to jump aboard. After experiencing your first ride on a steam locomotive, you're likely to forever feel delightful tingles racing down your spine each time you hear the melancholy moan of a far-off train whistle. It's an infectious feeling that you'll never want to lose.

Campground Information

Camping in the cinder-fever region is a special attraction by itself. Sprinkled about the entire area, you'll find a profusion of fine campgrounds, most of which are situated in attractive locations.

In Chama you can camp at the Rio Chama RV Park and Campground; (505) 756-2303. Just outside the city, you can choose between the 100-site, private Twin Rivers Campground and Trailer Park at the junction of U.S. 64, U.S. 84 and S.R. 17, or 25 miles southeast of U.S. 64, the 35-site La Isla Campground. Near Antonito, you'll find a number of national forest campgrounds, primarily west on S.R. 17. Here, you'll also have the choice of three private parks—Mogote Meadow, Ponderosa Camp and Twin Rivers Ranch.

Bordering Durango, seven private and four national forest campgrounds furnish scores of excellent sites with many more situated near Cortez, Mancos and Bayfield. During the summer these areas are extremely popular so, if possible, make advance reservations, or arrive early for first-come, first-served sites. By arranging a spring or autumn visit, you can avoid peak-season crowds and, as an added incentive, you'll find the mountains arrayed in a mantle of vivid colors.

Cinder Fever Facts

Attractive, illustrated mile-by-mile guide books are offered at all depots. Both *Cinders & Smoke,* the guide for the Durango to Silverton excursion, and *Ticket to Toltec,* the guide for the Cumbres & Toltec trip, are authored by Doris B. Osterwald and published by Western Guideways; $4.50.

Personalities

In Search of Quail

Searching for all six species of one of America's most popular game birds, a teacher turned writer fulfills a persistent dream

Tom Huggler

It was an old dream that recurred often, especially on October afternoons. While my high school students took their literature test, I'd look out the dusty windows of my classroom and think about driving across the country in a motorhome, my yellow Labrador and English setters in tow, stopping to hunt game birds whenever and wherever the opportunity presented itself. Then the students would hand in their papers, the bell would ring, my dream would drift away . . . for a while. Could I ever make it come true?

PHOTO: OUTDOOR IMAGES PHOTO/TOM HUGGLER

The author and his male setter with a pair of Mearns quail taken in southern Arizona near the Mexican border.

Five years ago I turned in my teacher's manuals and red-ink pens for a copy of *Writer's Market* and a word processor—tools of the freelancer's trade. A few months later, I found myself divorced and nearly broke, but free to travel and write and do what I wanted. Trips to Alaska and the American West provided photos and experiences for stories, but "The Dream," as I had come to think of it, was most persistent.

I settled on the quails of America for several reasons. First, they are the nation's second-most popular game bird—in terms of harvest—after the mourning dove. Hunters bag from 20 million to 30 million quail each year. Second, although we don't hunt them in my native Michigan,

Left, *Gambel quail, a handsome bird of the desert brushlands, is found in Arizona and New Mexico.* Right, *Bobwhites are hunted in 35 states.*

PHOTOS: OUTDOOR IMAGES PHOTO/TOM HUGGLER

the birds' northern habitat fringe, they are legal targets in 35 other states. Third, in addition to the popular bobwhite, there are five other huntable species of quail—none of which I had ever seen—in this country. Fourth, as near as I could tell, no one had ever collected all six on a single hunt.

I decided to start in the fall of 1985, but first, plenty of research and planning was in order. I wrote letters to state game and fish agencies to become familiar with hunting seasons, regulations, quail distribution and nonresident license costs. I also contacted fellow members of the Outdoor Writers Association of America to learn about hunting opportunities in their areas, and I spent nights pouring over maps and literature.

Once I had a working knowledge of what the hunting odyssey would involve, I began searching for a book publisher. A publisher's advance would help pay for some of the $3000 in expenses I expected to incur. Sales to magazines could also help recoup costs. Stackpole Books offered a contract, and several magazine editors expressed interest in my plans.

The next step was to line up a vehicle. My 1978 pickup had 120,000 miles and couldn't be trusted. Luckily, I was able to borrow a Winnebago LeSharo from friends. I sold the pickup, converting the $800 cash into gas for the motorhome. Although the manufacturer generally doesn't recommend towing a trailer with the four-cylinder LeSharo, my kennel-on-wheels weighed only 750 pounds loaded and had a minimal tongue weight. With the trailer in tow, I averaged nearly 16 mpg and experienced minimal, if any, difference in power, even while crossing the Continental Divide four times.

I decided on two trips rather than one. The first, which began on Halloween Eve and ended on Thanksgiving Day, took me to the Midwest. I hunted bobwhite quail in Iowa, Kansas, Oklahoma and Missouri and got my first look at scaled quail—fascinating game birds—in the grasslands of southwestern Kansas. On Christmas Day I headed out again, this time to the desert Southwest for western quail. Mindful that no one had bagged all six species of quail on a single trip, I hunted bobwhites again in Oklahoma, then scaled and Gambel quail in New Mexico and Arizona, the secretive Mearns quail in southern Arizona along the Mexican border, and valley and mountain quail in Nevada. I wheeled the rig back into my driveway on Superbowl Sunday. During the two trips I had driven 13,000 miles and, as near as I could figure it, had walked about 300 miles behind my dogs.

Was it worth the effort and expense? Well, as I write this, I am looking at six mounted cock quail on a skeleton of cholla cactus that I picked up in the Sonoran Desert in Arizona. But lest you think this "hunt of a lifetime" was a bloodbath of shooting quail, let me assure you that I killed only what I planned to eat in the motorhome, have mounted or

On the upper Sonoran Desert in central New Mexico, game is scarce, partly due to lack of water.

give away to my hosts—farmers and landowners who gave me permission to hunt—or to friends who sometimes accompanied me on public land. And there were many days when I carried only cameras and a note pad and pencil.

In many respects, the hunting was a reward because I was working on a fishing book and trying to keep up with magazine assignments and forwarded correspondence, during my travels. A typical day would begin at 5 or 6 A.M. I'd plug in the coffee pot and write on my word processor (the motorhome was equipped with a generator) until midmorning or later. As any quail hunter knows, the birds offer a gentleman's sport. Leisurely hunting during banker's hours is as productive as busting heavy covers all day. So I would hunt in the middle hours of the day, then drive a few hours to my next location—a state park, farmer's driveway or home of a friend. Usually, I'd cook supper in the motorhome while sipping a drink, then bring in the dogs one at a time for companionship and to check them over for cockleburs, cacti spines and cuts. Later I might clean guns, boots and cameras, then enter the day's experiences and observations into the tape recorder I used as a journal.

Bob Hirsch (left) talks with spectator while hunting in Arizona.

PHOTO: OUTDOOR IMAGES PHOTO/TOM HUGGLER

The hunting was also a bonus to the wide range of experiences I enjoyed and people I met. I think back now to the Kansas farmer who was down on his luck. Dick was 32, his wife, Sally, 26, and their five children looked like a stair-step family. Farm income is at an all-time low for such family farmers. The $1.55-per-hundredweight that Dick received for his milo was the same price his father got in 1955. I ate government welfare cheese at their table, and I helped Dick jumpstart his battered grain truck with the 1948 vintage license plate. I like to think one of the brightest days of that disastrous fall for him was helping me find some bobwhite coveys on his rental property.

A week later I was hunting on a 5,000-acre Oklahoma ranch, owned by a family that suddenly had become millionaires, thanks to the discovery of oil on their land. After a fine opening day, when four of us bagged limits of ten bobwhites each, we ate delicious barbecued ribs at the ranchhouse, a mansion with wall-to-wall ceramic tile. "These are the best ribs I've ever eaten," I told my host. "Where do you get such wonderful sauce?"

"Welllll," he drawled, "ya'll have to buy a chain of restaurants to get that sauce."

It was a wonderful way to see and feel America, both through the accelerator pedal and the tightness of my legs from miles and miles of driving and walking. Besides the people I met, I experienced bitter cold on the plains of Kansas, three steady days of rain in Missouri, the dry heat of a desert at high noon and shortness of breath at 10,000-foot altitude. I saw the bigness of our country—the muted patchwork of color, painted by the artist's sweeping brush from horizon to horizon, and the farm combines at dusk, looking like three-eyed alien insects with their headlights and cutter-bar light on, crawling through the fields.

And I saw the small things—crumbling lespideza in my hands and picking out the tiny seeds that quail so love. At dawn one morning in Missouri, I lay in the motorhome and listened to a farm dog barking in the distance, then heard the "clack, clack" of freight-train wheels pounding a loose tie on the Kansas City Southern Railway.

I could not have seen and heard those things from a classroom. Strange how the common denominator for those experiences was a six-ounce game bird.

I learned, for example, that unlike pheasants and some other game birds, the quails are monogamous. The "bob-bob-white" whistles that we hear in the spring along brushy fence rows and from farm fields are the desperation calls of unmated males. I learned that the reason these fragile birds can't survive in deep snow and sustained cold is because of their high metabolic rate.

That's why three weekends of terrible winter storms in January 1977 wiped out ninety-five percent of Ohio's and Michigan's bobwhite populations. They are just now coming back. On the other hand, in states where they are plentiful, quails are most resilient. Combined losses from hunting, predation and the elements can knock their numbers down by seventy percent, yet the birds will rebound in a single year.

The western species intrigued me, and my dogs, too. I learned that I couldn't outrun the scaled quail, which lives in semiarid grasslands and is unusual looking with its scalelike belly feathering and crested head sporting a white tuft at the top like some punk rocker. Scaled quail often share habitat edges with the Gambel quail, a handsome bird of the desert brushlands with a rust-colored crown and comma-like head feather drooping over all. Mearns quail, a colorful bird with black-and-white polka-dot breast, gave my dogs fits in its mountain habitat of grasslands interspersed with oaks. In such open country my setters, Lady Macbeth and Chaucer (what else would a former English teacher name his English setters?), run fast and hard. Because Mearns, which are also called harlequin (clownlike) or Montezuma quails, are squatters and exude little scent, the hard-charging dogs ran right over them.

Valley or California quails were frustrating, too, especially when they ran ahead of us, in coveys of up to sixty birds, then hid in thick greasebrush along ranchland irrigation ditches and refused to fly. Mountain quails were the supreme challenge, and so I hunted Holly, my yellow Labrador, with the setters. We had to go to 7,000-foot altitude in the Pine Nut Mountains between Nevada and California, and during four days of hunting collected only two birds. Bagging one of these elusive quails with the featherlike plume, however, meant that my dream had come true.

Now I have another dream. My research on quail uncovered interesting facts about another game bird, the grouse. I learned, for example, that grouse and quail were likely the same bird some 25 million years ago, but that they split along evolutionary lines—the quails having their speciation to the south, mostly in Central and South America, and the grouse moving north to occupy precise habitat niches around the globe. The ruffed grouse is the most popular of the seven native species living in America, but, to my knowledge, no hunter has collected them all on a single trip.

Why have dreams in the first place, if there is no possibility of them ever coming true?

Fishing for Dollars

When Jerry Wood packs his fishing gear into his RV, he's off to work

Jim Zumbo

Jerry Wood is a lucky man. He loves his work. Not many people are in that enviable situation.

Wood works from a bass boat and catches fish for a living. No, he doesn't sell what he catches—he competes with other anglers in tournaments and wins money by placing high in nationwide competitions.

Bass tournaments are catching on like wildfire across America. The idea was born in the south in the 1960s, and now every state has avid followers. The West Coast was slow to catch the fever at first, but now western states, especially California, present a force to be reckoned with in national events.

Jerry Wood started fishing as a youngster when he frequently visited his grandmother on the Texas coast. She owned a resort, and young Wood made some spare change catching and selling bait to guests.

Wood took a job with a utility company and joined its employees' bass club. He met Jack Lewis, a well-known angler famous for using the spinnerbait—a lure that has a lead head, spinners and bright plastic streamers. Lewis took Wood under his wing and taught him bass basics.

Now Wood's favorite lure is the spinnerbait. "Most tournaments are won in shallow water," he explained, "and often in streams or river inlets where the water is somewhat discolored. That's where the spinnerbait works best, and I have a lot of faith in it."

In 1974, Wood moved to Albuquerque, New Mexico, where he worked as a representative for a clothing firm. There were few bass lakes in the area, but he enjoyed trout fishing in the high country. Shortly afterward, he moved to Tulsa and promptly joined the Okie Bassbusters Club. He started fishing the International Bass Association and Poor Boy circuits, and easily qualified for major tournaments.

At this time the prestigious B.A.S.S. organization changed its rules, which allowed Wood to compete in its tournaments. B.A.S.S. no longer

PHOTO: JIM ZUMBO

Motorhomes can launch boats anywhere there's a ramp, including most lakes.

required contestants to qualify in six national tournaments, a rule which precluded Wood from participating because of the travel involved. The new regulations divided the circuit into east and west, allowing anglers to fish in three qualifying events for eligibility in the Classic—the most renowned major fishing tournament in the United States. Until then, Wood's job kept him from fishing as much as he wanted, and he fished only when his work schedule permitted.

In 1984 he finished a full year on the circuit, and in 1985 he did well enough to be considered for the Angler of the Year award. In 1986, Wood was able to fish full time on the tournament trail.

"I love to fish for the sheer enjoyment of the sport," Wood said, "but my competitive nature drives me a bit, whether I'm fishing a tournament or not. And, of course, when a company sponsors me, I do my best to excel just because they have faith in my abilities."

Jerry Wood's life-style demands mobility. He travels across the country from one tournament to the next, and during peak months is on the road in his RV more than he's home. That's why he's a happy convert to the RV lifestyle.

It's nothing for Wood to make long-distance trips on the tournament trail. Last year, for example, he drove from Tulsa, Oklahoma, to northern New York to compete in a fishing event.

"My motorhome reduces travel costs considerably," Wood said. "That's the major benefit of using it. When we go to tournaments, some of the events are based in expensive hotels. The cost of a room eats into my profit, but my RV helps eliminate those expenses.

"Food is also a big expense," Wood continued. "By cooking in my motorhome, I can eat what I want whenever I want, and keep my food budget nicely trimmed. And if I just want a bologna sandwich, I dig around in the refrigerator and make one. It would be easy to spend $200 or more on food during a week-long tournament by eating in restaurants.

PHOTOS: JIM ZUMBO

Left, *Wood lands a fine largemouth bass during a fishing tournament.* Upper right, *Jerry Wood sorts tackle outside his motorhome. He likes the storage capability, which allows him to bring backup tackle on tournament trips.* Lower right, *Tension is high during the official weigh-in, after which tournament prizes of up to $100,000 are awarded.*

For about $50, I can buy groceries and do my own cooking."

Another benefit of the motorhome, according to Wood, is that it allows him to stay close to the boat ramp, where the contestants start in the morning. "I can get more rest by parking my motorhome near the lake and overnighting there," Wood explained. "Proper rest is important, and I don't have to get up extra early to leave the hotel. All I need to do is get out of bed, make some coffee, and walk down to the boat."

Every tournament angler will agree that proper rest is vital. While fishing, the contestant must be mentally alert. Concentration is important, not only to determine where the fish might be and what they'll strike, but to be able to react quickly when a fish hits the lure.

Another requirement for professional anglers is the need to be properly psyched before and during an event.

"I like to be around people," Wood said, "but prior to a competition I want to be alone to mentally prepare. If you're in a motel, other fishermen are apt to come by to visit and discuss how many fish they caught, what they caught them on, and other details. That's fine, but I'd rather be by myself and stick to my own game plan. It's easy to get confused and lose sight of your strategy by talking to people. What works for one angler doesn't necessarily work for others. My motorhome gives me the privacy I want during this time of mental preparation."

Because of the long trips involved in driving to tournaments, Wood likes the idea of pulling over and resting whenever he's tired. "I don't have to worry about getting to a motel and wondering if there's a room available," he said. "And when I reach my destination, I can simply pull in and sleep, cook or do whatever I need to without the bother of checking into a room.

"My motorhome has become my second home," Wood said. "I like sleeping in my own bed. It's my place, where I can be more comfortable and rest better. This might sound funny, and I've said it to many people, but when I get up in the morning, I know where my socks are."

Tournament anglers own a great deal of fishing tackle so they're prepared for any eventuality. Wood says his RV allows him to carry a lot of tackle and to keep it well organized. "My motorhome has plenty of space, permitting me to keep my tackle neat and sorted. I don't like it jammed up in a small area, which would be the case if I didn't have an RV. The extra space also allows me to store back-up tackle that I might need to use in a tournament. For example, maybe the bass are hitting a purple something really well, and I lose that lure. There are more in my motorhome, so I don't have to worry about running to a sporting-goods store to find an identical lure.

"Finally," Wood said, "the motorhome offers a fine tax advantage. Since I fish for a living, I got an investment credit when I purchased the motorhome. And, of course, my RV travel expenses are deductible."

How popular are motorhomes with tournament anglers? According to observers involved in the sport, each year there are more motorhomes on the fishing circuits. The ability to tow a bass boat makes a motorhome well suited to the professional traveling fisherman. And the homelike amenities of a motorhome offer other advantages that fit in quite nicely with this angling lifestyle.

Obviously, Jerry Wood believes his motorhome is an important component of life on the tournament circuit, and other fishermen are catching on to that fact as well.

Our Season in the Sun

Three months on the road touring the natural wonders of the West brought this young couple closer to the land and each other

Bill Poss

Authors Bill and Kate Poss pose at Lower Yellowstone Falls in Yellowstone National Park, Wyoming.

PHOTOS: KATE POSS

With a little patience and faith, even your wildest dreams can come true. For many years my wife Kate and I had fantasized about taking off for a few months to travel throughout the American West. A fantasy indeed, but we kept the idea in the back of our minds.

Perhaps the initial inspiration for such an adventure came from my grandparents. They had countless stories (and slides) of their trailer trips across America and Mexico during the 1950s and 1960s. Although retired for medical reasons, their spirit of adventure had opened up a whole new world for them. But how could we, in our early 30s, find the time to travel as they did?

We had always loved camping in our tent, thinking trailers were for retired folks. After numerous encounters with inclement weather, however, my grandparents' praises of trailering began to make sense. Stormy weather rarely shortened their trips or forced them into hotels.

Our curiosity about trailers began to grow. Parked in the storage yard of our mobile-home park was a trailer that appeared to be the type we might enjoy. We noticed that it sat there for months without being used. One day I noticed a small card on our clubhouse bulletin board: "Travel Trailer for Sale."

Was it just a coincidence or fate? After inspecting the trailer, we knew

At Zion National Park, Utah, the remote subway formation was awesome.

that was the one for us. It is an older trailer (1966 Cardinal), but in excellent condition. Only 13 feet long and 6 feet high, every square inch is engineered for space and comfort. What really sold us, though, was its wood interior. The ceiling, cabinets and walls are made of real wood. Although heavier than modern trailers, the cozy cabin ambiance was worth the extra pounds to us.

We christened her "Carmen the Gypsy" and began our introduction into the world of trailering. After a few weekend trips, we realized that this would be the way to travel comfortably and inexpensively for an extended period of time.

But how could we get away?

One day in December 1985, the answer came. I could make an anticipated career change and leave my current job three months before starting a new position with a private engineering firm. Kate could have someone cover her job in group health insurance while she was away. Now we seriously considered what a short while ago had been only a dream.

Although we managed to set aside the three months from work, we still had obstacles to overcome. Most important was finding the right person to house-sit for us. We needed someone we could trust with our home and to care for our two cats.

With nearly a month until our planned departure date, we still hadn't found anyone. We were afraid the trip would fall through when suddenly a neighbor introduced his close friend, who had recently been separated and needed a place to live. The moment we met, we knew he was the right one.

The vehicle we use to tow our trailer is "Olga," a 1979 Volvo sedan. Although she has only a four-cylinder engine, previous trips proved she could tow Carmen quite well. We move slowly up hills, but without any problems. The equalizing hitch is a big help.

Olga already had more than 150,000 miles, but had always run well. However, a complete inspection uncovered some very necessary repairs, including new brakes, clutch, hoses, belts, water pump and thermostat. When we saw the list of repairs, we wondered if Olga could make such a long journey, but we couldn't afford a new vehicle and take the trip, too. After some agonizing analyses, we decided to have the repairs made and put our faith in Olga. Our decision paid off; she ran strong throughout the trip.

While planning to be on the road for three months, we thought of all

PHOTO: KATE POSS

Home-base camping at Atherton Creek Campground in the Teton National Forest allowed authors the opportunity to hike, bicycle, and explore area.

kinds of things to bring. However we wanted to tow as little weight as possible, which made for some critical choices. Our clothing ranged from shorts and sandals to long-johns and woolens. Other necessities included snow chains, tools, extra hoses and belts, shovel, ax, first-aid kit, battery-powered radio and our solar shower (an ingenious device we used often).

Hiking mountain trails at Atherton, the Posses captured Wyoming's mighty Tetons on film.

PHOTOS: KATE POSS

During all the years we dreamed of such a trip, we saved as much money as we could, in case the opportunity ever arose. Surprisingly, a three-month trailer trip is not as expensive as might be imagined. Of course, we had to be sure all our bills and mortgage were paid in advance. Our philosophy is to travel simply and basically. We avoid expensive tours and high-priced meals and just enjoy the wide-open spaces.

From the information we received, we figured campground fees at an average of $5 per night. National parks are a little higher and national forests a little less. On many public lands camping is free but primitive (bring your own water and pack out your trash).

We calculated our food costs slightly lower than our weekly budget at home, since we would eat most of our meals in our trailer. We planned to load up on supplies in the larger towns before heading into more remote areas, where prices are higher.

Fortunately, gasoline prices were the lowest they'd been in years. We figured an average of $1 per gallon. Our car gets about 12-15 mpg when towing and about 20-25 mpg on her own. We came up with a very rough estimate of $500 for gas and propane.

After including costs for gifts, laundry, postage, film and miscellaneous items, we figured a grand total of $2,500 with $500 extra. (It turned out to be an accurate estimate; we spent almost exactly $3,000 or $1,000 a month.)

We began to pour over every available book, magazine and map we could find about the west. Some of the best maps and information we received came from the national parks and and national forests in the western states.

Eventually we settled on a basic plan. We would head north from our Southern California home to the cool mountains of Idaho and Montana during August. In September we would travel south through Wyoming, Utah and southwestern Colorado. In October we would follow the fall weather into New Mexico and Arizona, then return home.

Suddenly the months of planning and anticipation were over. The first of August had finally arrived. Although we were very excited, I have to admit I was a little scared. It was hard to believe we would be gone for three months.

After two and a half days of steady driving, we arrived in the Sawtooth Mountains of southwestern Idaho. The cool mountain air was a relief from the desert heat we had driven through. We set up camp in a national forest campground on the banks of the Salmon River, a few miles east of the small town of Stanley.

Despite the area's spectacular natural beauty, there are no crowds of people or fast-food joints there. Most folks come to fish, float the Salmon, hike in the mountains or just relax. We didn't do any fishing, but our friendly campground neighbor shared his bountiful daily catch with us.

Bicycling in Zion National Park on a warm, fall day was exhilarating.

We took some day hikes into the Sawtooth Mountains instead.

The Stanley-Sawtooth area has a long history of adventurous pioneers seeking a way of life from the land. The local museum's curator, Edna McGown, told us how the rich valley attracted fur trappers, miners, lumbermen and ranchers. The remote valley and its severe winters challenged the stoutest settlers. We visited the nearby mining town of Custer. Many of the 1800s buildings are intact and have been designated as historical sites.

After a week in the area, we felt the urge to move northward. On our last evening in Stanley we sat on the wooden porch at Casanova Jack's Rod and Gun Club, listening to Jack and friends play guitars and sing songs. It was hard to leave, but we knew there was so much ahead waiting to be discovered.

We drove north along the Salmon River, then over the mountains and into Montana. We were amazed by the vastness of this country, with its miles of forests, ranches and wheat fields.

After loading up with fresh supplies in Missoula, Montana, we drove on to Glacier National Park. We slowly pulled Carmen over the dizzying heights of Going-to-the-Sun Highway and made camp at the Rising Sun Campground.

Glacier Park is a stunning piece of American wilderness. At Logan Pass, near the visitors center, we hiked through an alpine meadow covered with wildflowers. The delicate blooms last only a few weeks on these windswept mountains. We sat down in the meadow, surrounded by the massive mountains, and became intoxicated by the beauty there. Couldn't we bottle up this feeling and take it with us to open whenever needed?

Along this same trail a few days later, we had another magical experience. We were sitting on a rock eating lunch when a white figure emerged from the trees. We sat motionless, watching a handsome mountain goat saunter up to within ten feet of us! He casually grazed the nearby grasses, then sat down in the shade of some trees. He didn't seem to mind us staring at him in awe.

We spent a week in the area, hiking in the mountains almost every day. With all that exercise and fresh air, we felt invigorated. It was so rewarding to share this much time with each other. We didn't even think of television and hadn't heard a phone ring in more than two weeks. We had brought along a good selection of books and kept a journal of our adventures along the way.

We stayed another week in Glacier Park in the Many Glacier Valley. Only hard-sided camping trailers are allowed there due to the close proximity of grizzly bears.

George, a retired gentleman, brought his spotting scope over to our campsite a couple of nights. Looking through it, we saw mountain goats, bighorn sheep and a grizzly bear on the mountainsides. George told us that he spends his summers in Glacier and loves every inch of the park.

In addition to the wilderness experiences, we found entertainment at the nearby Many Glacier Hotel. This European-style hotel, built in 1915 by the Great Northern Railroad, is staffed with college students during the summer. Six nights a week they perform in a variety of musical shows in the hotel's huge lobby. The opportunity to perform and work in Glacier Park draws talented students from across the country.

During the last few days of August, a cold wind blew in from the north. The aspens and willows were beginning to turn yellow and gold. Fall comes very early in northern Montana, so we decided to head south.

After hearing so many differing opinions about Yellowstone, we decided to see it for ourselves. It wasn't overcrowded; we found a campsite easily. However, most visitors congregate at the same places along the roadways. We found that once we got off the roads, the park seemed almost empty. Of course, we enjoyed the main features, such as Old Faithful and Yellowstone Falls, but our most rewarding times were hikes to Fairy Falls, Imperial Geyser and to the top of Mount Washburn.

Thanks to John D. Rockefeller Jr., Horace Albright (one of the founders of the National Park Service) and others, another jewel of America's heritage has been preserved. Grand Teton National Park originally consisted of only the mountains and the small lakes at its base. Rockefeller's gift added the entire Snake River Valley with its abundant wildlife. Perhaps the most famous vista in the American West is the view across the Snake River to the Grand Tetons.

We arrived just after Labor Day weekend, and the park was nearly empty. Our two weeks there were perhaps the high point of our journey. We camped just outside the park boundary in the Teton National Forest. From there we explored the park, hiking in the Tetons and bicycling through the Snake River Valley.

We made a habit of concluding each day's adventure with a rootbeer float at the Slide Inn in Kelly (a small community inside the park). It was there we met Bill and Sylvia, a couple who had recently moved there from Texas. We became close friends and shared some unforgettable experiences. They took us four-wheeling deep into the Teton National Forest to breathtaking mountaintop vistas. We drank coffee and told stories in their tent while a booming thunderstorm rolled by. One night they invited us over for a fresh fish dinner. Kate served an apple pie she had baked in our trailer's stovetop oven. That night we sat around their campfire, sharing our hopes and dreams.

We felt so comfortable and at home that we wanted to stay longer. However, we were halfway through our three-month trip already and still had a long way to go.

With the season's first snowfall on our heels, we traveled south toward southeastern Utah. An entirely different world greeted us there. It is a high desert of massive red sandstone and deep canyons. This had always been one of my grandparents' favorite places; we soon learned the reason.

We camped for a week on a secluded beach at the edge of the Colorado River near Moab. Vertical walls of sandstone rise above the far side of the river. The days were warm, almost hot, and the nights balmy. We sat around the fire each night in shorts and T-shirts, watching the harvest moon illuminate the canyon walls. It was there we learned about juniper, the twisted tree that grows out of the sandstone. The hot desert sun dries the fallen wood to perfection. In a campfire, it burns clean and hot with a sweet fragrance.

We explored the canyons of the Colorado River and the strange rock formations of nearby Arches National Park. Most impressive was Delicate Arch, a natural work of art perched on the brink of a canyon.

By coincidence, some friends were in Moab at the same time we were. We shared our campfire and Kate's baked goodies one night, and they had us over to their trailer for dinner the following night.

Fall had officially arrived, but the temperature was still warm. A few days later, this changed dramatically. As we pulled into a campground in the San Juan Mountains of southwestern Colorado, a snowstorm was under way. Although it snowed on and off for the next couple of days, we stayed warm in Carmen, even though we had no electrical hookups. Our propane lantern generated an amazing amount of heat, and we did a lot of cooking. When the sun finally returned, it was a glorious scene. The aspens were blazing gold and the mountains covered with snow. We visited the historic mining towns of Telluride and Silverton before heading south to New Mexico.

In early October, we arrived in Taos, New Mexico. This ancient town is located in the high desert at the foot of the Sangre de Cristo Mountains. One of the oldest settlements in the United States, Taos has an interesting blend of cultures. Indian, Spanish and Anglo people have lived there for centuries. More recently, Taos has become an artists' colony with dozens of galleries and museums. Our visit coincided with the annual arts festival, a week-long celebration of exhibits, gallery openings, music and craft fairs.

Autumn is a colorful time to be in Taos. The sun casts a golden light on the adobe buildings and cottonwood trees. Red chile *ristras* hang from porches, and apples and piñon nuts are sold at roadside stands.

We camped along the Don Fernando River about four miles east of the Taos Plaza. From there we rode our bicycles into town, always stopping at the La Vineteria spring to fill our water bottles.

In the mountain country of northern New Mexico lie a number of small villages that seem to be from another century. Each has its own adobe church with a bell tower and three crosses. Our favorite town was Chimayo, where we met Leona. She and her husband own a small RV park, café and tortilla factory. Her food was the freshest and the tastiest we've ever eaten.

The pleasant Indian summer weather we enjoyed in Taos suddenly changed on us. We were returning to our trailer in the Jemez Mountains after a day of visiting Santa Fe's art galleries when a fierce blizzard began. The snow was blowing so hard, we could hardly see the road. We put on our chains and slowly drove into the mountains to Carmen. The next morning we awoke to more than a foot of snow covering everything. It was a beautiful sight.

The radio warned of more heavy snowfall coming, however, so we decided to pull out. Even with snow chains on, our tires spun helplessly as we tried to pull Carmen up a hill to the highway. Suddenly one chain broke and flew off the tire. We dug a path through the snow, and we made it onto the highway, but our muffler then cracked loose and the driver's-side window fell down. When it rains (or snows), it pours.

We drove into Albuquerque and hooked up at the Palisades RV Park. After a couple of days, all repairs were reasonably made.

From there we headed west. We had become very attached to New Mexico and were reluctant to leave. Westbound on Interstate 40, we stopped at the small town of Thoreau. Here we discovered an outdoor sculpture exhibit at the Carol Sayer Gallery. Carol's husband, Jim, guided us through the exhibit, telling stories about each piece and its creator. Our mutual passion for New Mexico was reflected in his eyes and voice: "It's more than a good feeling here," he said, "it's magic!"

At this point, only two weeks of our trip remained. We were so used to living this way that we wondered how we would adjust to "normal" life back home.

We drove on to Sedona, Arizona, where we met Kate's sister from Las Vegas and her cousin from Phoenix. We camped together for a few days, enjoying the family reunion. Kate and I lingered a few more days after they left. Sedona is surrounded by magnificent red-rock formations and its temperate climate has attracted artists, writers and retirees.

With only a week left for our trip, we drove north toward Lake Powell, on the Arizona-Utah border. The rangers there told us of a secluded, primitive camping area called Lone Rock. We camped there overnight at the edge of the lake. The air was warm and the placid water invited us in for a quick swim.

We also visited Paria Canyon Primitive Area, west of Lake Powell, on Bureau of Land Management (BLM) property. While in Jackson, Wyoming, we had seen an exhibit of photographs taken in this area. After we had described the photos to the BLM ranger, he suggested we hike the Buckskin Gulch trail. The trail is actually a dry streambed for about a mile, then suddenly drops into a deep and narrow canyon. Once we climbed down inside, we realized we were where the photos had been taken. The passageway was only about 5 feet wide with vertical walls more than 100 feet high. The sandstone has been scalloped by the force of water, creating a bizarre labryinth. Although the sun was shining above, it was almost dark down at the bottom. We hiked through the strange maze until our way was blocked by a pool of water, before turning back.

On our way to Zion National Park, we stopped in the town of Hurricane to visit Pah Tempe Hot Springs. The hot mineral water flows into several pools at the edge of the Virgin River. We soaked in it one evening, watching the shooting stars streak across the sky.

Zion was the ideal place to conclude our journey. We found very few people there, balmy Indian summer weather and miles of excellent hiking trails. There, too, the trees wore peak fall colors. During those last nights we stayed up late by the campfire, trying to extend each day.

What I'll miss most of all is the time we were able to spend together. The unhurried time to talk and listen and just be together is hard to come by when we're at home. We had three months of rising in the morning and not going our separate ways. Although the trip is over now, the closeness we have shared will always be with us.

Technical

Maintenance Plus:

The Energy Source

Electrical power must be stored to start or operate nearly everything in a motorhome, so it's good to know how to keep them trouble-free

Brian Robertson

The lead-acid storage battery contains an amazing amount of energy, considering its size and weight. Capable of starting a coach engine thousands of times, in all kinds of weather, year after year, it's truly an amazing device.

Normally taken for granted, the battery is the heart of a motorhome's vital functions. Poor maintenance and neglect lead batteries to early graves, while proper care will provide many years of reliable service.

Inspection

Frequent battery inspection can prevent problems by spotting trouble areas before they get out of hand. It's a good idea to make a habit of checking the battery whenever the hood is raised. Areas to check include the battery cables, electrolyte level, battery posts and terminals, battery case and the battery hold-down bracket.

If your battery is not maintenance free, electrolyte-level checks are important, especially in hot weather when battery gassing is heaviest. Heat causes the electrolyte level to drop more rapidly. If cell plates become exposed to the air, rapid deterioration of the plates will occur. If water is needed to bring the electrolyte level up, make sure you use a pure distilled water; tap water contains chemicals and minerals that can shorten a battery's life.

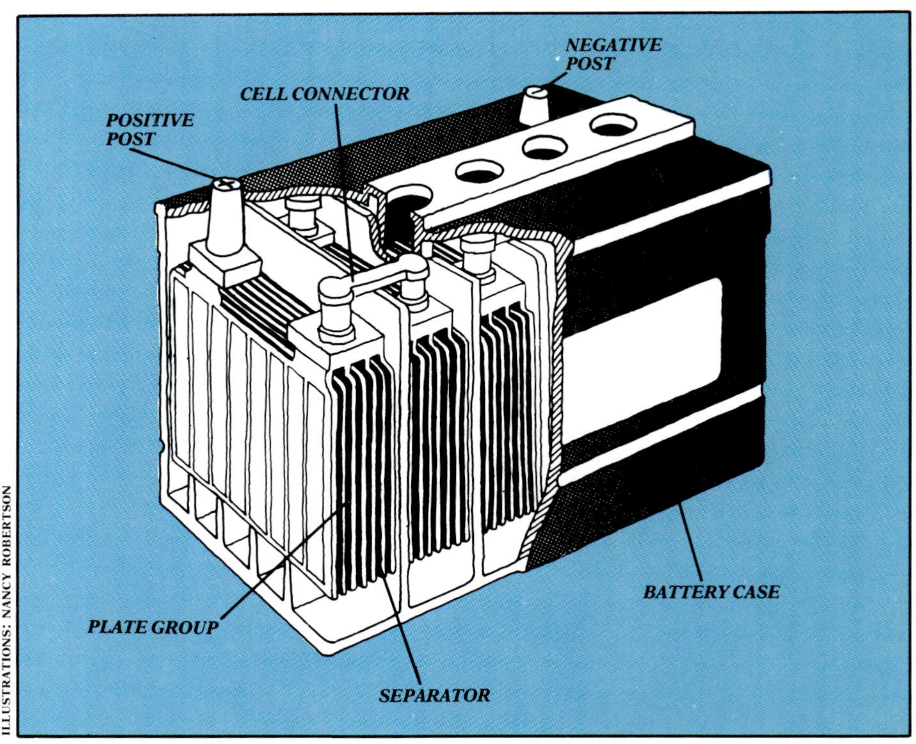

ILLUSTRATIONS: NANCY ROBERTSON

Safety Tip: Battery gassing releases hydrogen gas, which is extremely flammable. Never smoke, expose an open flame or create sparks around a battery; it can explode!

Check battery cables for worn, cracked insulation. Replace any cable that is suspect. Cable terminals and battery posts should be checked for corrosion. Many a battery has been incorrectly condemned due to the resistance caused by poor terminal-to-post connections.

The battery case should be checked for cracks. In order to thoroughly inspect the case, it's a good idea to remove the battery from the hold-down bracket and battery box. Batteries are heavy, so to reduce chances of dropping one or hurting your knuckles, use a battery carrier to lift the unit from its box.

To remove the battery, it's necessary to remove the cable terminals. Make sure that you use a box-end wrench of the correct size to remove the terminal nut. If the terminal is stuck on the post, use a battery-cable puller. Excessive prying or hammering on cable terminals can break off the soft-lead battery post, rendering the battery useless.

With the battery out of the box, wash all four sides and the bottom with baking soda and water. Corrosion is easily removed by using an old paintbrush dipped in a solution of baking soda and water. (Use about one-half cup of baking soda to one quart of water.) Vigorously scrub the terminals and battery top, then rinse with clean water. Be careful not to get the cleaning solution in the cells, as it will neutralize the electrolyte.

After all corrosion is removed, you can get a good look at the terminals and determine if there is any damage. Terminals that are eaten away badly by corrosion should be replaced with new terminals. Check for signs of cracks or wear-through caused by a loose hold-down. A crack or hole in the case of the battery calls for immediate replacement.

While the battery is disconnected, give the terminals and posts a good cleaning. Use a special battery brush or other type of post/terminal cleaning tool to clean the inside of the terminal and the outside of the post. A thin layer of petroleum jelly (Vaseline) applied to the posts and terminals will reduce the rate of corrosion.

Make sure the battery hold-down keeps the battery rigidly in its tray. A loose battery is susceptible to vibration damage, which causes plate

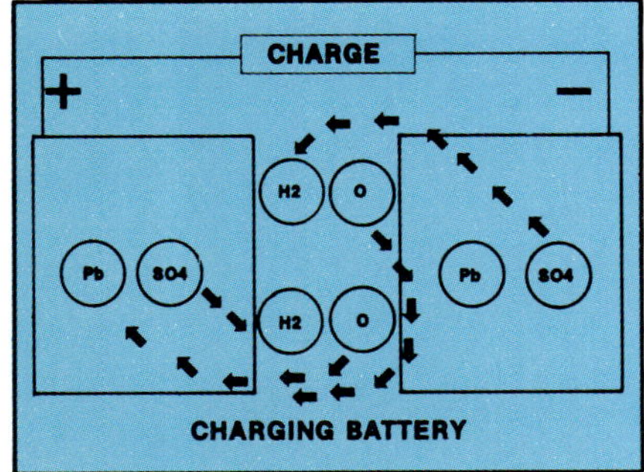

By charging the battery, acid strength is increased. This increases the specific gravity, resulting in a greater potential for chemical action to take place between the plates.

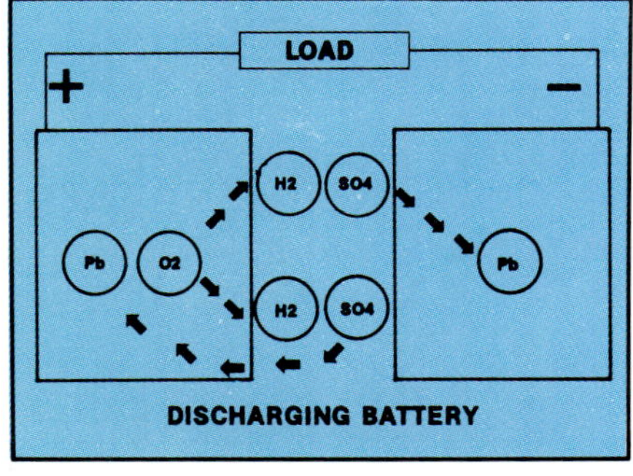

When a load is applied to a battery, the components of sulfuric acid (electrolyte) are separated. This reduction in acid strength decreases the battery's reserve capacity.

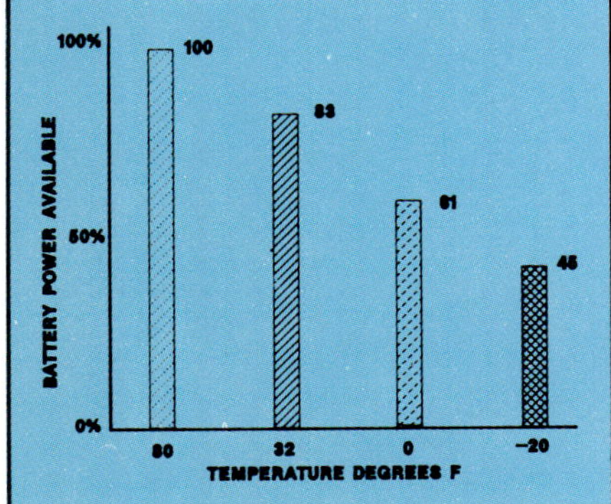

Low temperatures slow the chemical reaction and the battery's ability to provide electrical power. At 80°F, the battery has 100% of its power available, at −20°, a battery can produce only 45% of its capacity.

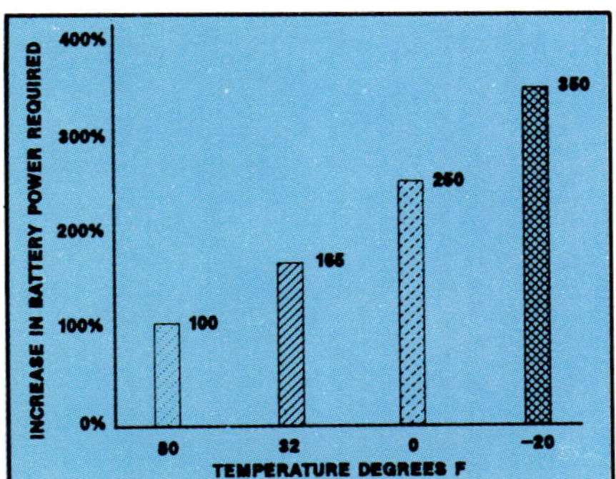

A motorhome engine places great demands on the battery in cold weather. Considering a battery is only 45% effective (see chart at left) at −20°, and the engine requires 350% more cranking power, it may be tough to get going!

material to shed. This, in turn, reduces the potential for chemical reaction. The hold-down rods, nuts, washers, bracket and battery box can be cleaned with baking soda solution and inspected. Worn or broken parts should be replaced.

Battery testing is a vital part of automotive electronic diagnosis. With today's computer-controlled electronics, a consistent supply of electrical power is mandatory. A marginal battery can render a motorhome helpless.

Specific Gravity Tests

The measurement of electrolyte-specific gravity has long been used as an indicator of a battery's state of charge. But, with the new maintenance-free batteries that have sealed cells, testing electrolyte is impossible, and other tests must be used. For those batteries that have cell openings, specific gravity tests are still valid.

Specific gravity is measured with a hydrometer. When measured, pure water has a specific gravity of 1.000. The electrolyte in a fully charged battery at 80°F will read up to 1.280, or 1.28 times heavier than pure water. The accompanying chart shows specific gravity ranges and the corresponding states of charge.

Specific gravity readings must be taken carefully, as temperature plays a role. For every 10 degrees that the electrolyte is above 80, you must add .004 to the reading; for every 10 degrees below 80, you subtract

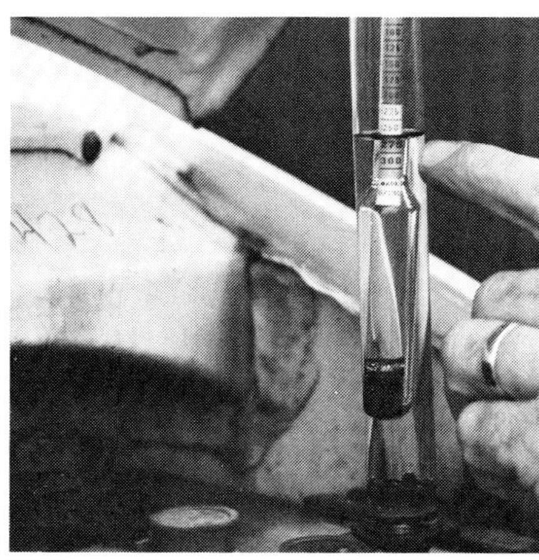

Left, ***Tools for proper battery care are not expensive, but sure make life easier when it comes to working on that vital part of your vehicle.*** **Right,** ***A hydrometer is used to test the specific gravity of the battery's electrolyte, which indicates the level of charge.***

.004. Variation between cells can be measured to detect a bad cell. Generally, if a variation of more than 50 points (.050) between cells exists, the battery is probably defective and will not hold a charge. While specific gravity is a good indicator of the state of charge, it is not a good indicator of the battery's capacity to do work; for this we need yet another test.

Load or Capacity Test

Applying a load test to a battery separates the good from the bad very quickly. The best method for load testing is to use a battery-testing machine, which simulates a high amperage draw, much like that of the engine's starter motor, to rapidly discharge the battery.

The tester is set to draw a load on the battery at half its cold cranking rating for 15 seconds. At the end of the 15-second period, the voltage is read on a voltmeter. If a battery is up to snuff, the voltage should not fall below 9.6 volts. Performance of less than this indicates an internal defect in the battery, making it a good candidate for replacement.

You can perform your own load test by removing the battery lead to the coil or the HEI distributor cap. Have a helper crank the engine for 15 seconds, while you watch the voltmeter. At the end of 15 seconds, the voltage should be above 9.6; if it's not, it's time for a new battery. *Caution:* Repeated, prolonged cranking can damage starter motors, so don't overdo it!

Batteries: Portable Power

The battery converts chemical energy to electrical energy by means of dissimilar types of lead, held on plates by a wire grid and submerged in a solution of sulfuric acid and water, more commonly called electrolyte. It's the chemical reaction between the active material on the plates and the sulfuric acid of the electrolyte that creates the electrical energy. The amount of electrical energy that a battery can produce is limited by the active area, the weight of the plate material and the strength of the sulphuric acid.

As electrical energy is used from the battery, a chemical reaction reduces the electrolyte. The battery is now discharged. Before the battery can be used again, it must be recharged by receiving direct current. The charge flows to the battery in the opposite direction of the current during discharge. This reverses the job of the engine's charging system, the chemical reaction and restores the acidity to the electrolyte.

Construction

Lead-acid storage battery construction is fairly simple. The basic building blocks are the battery grids. Grids are lattice-like lead castings with vertical and horizontal wires surrounded by a border that supports this

PHOTOS: NANCY ROBERTSON

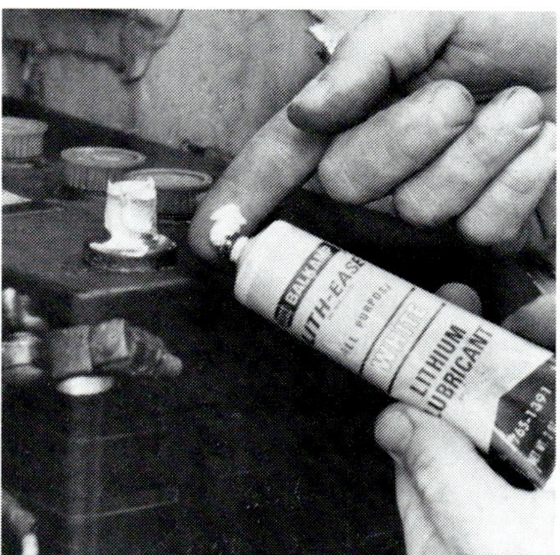

Left, ***Periodic cleaning of battery terminals should be done to insure optimum conductance of voltage through the battery leads.*** **Right,** ***A light coating of lithium lubricant on the battery terminals will inhibit corrosion.***

SPECIFIC GRAVITY READING	BATTERY CONDITION
1.260 – 1.280	FULLY CHARGED
1.230 – 1.250	3/4 CHARGED
1.200 – 1.220	1/2 CHARGED
1.170 – 1.190	VERY LITTLE POWER
1.110 – 1.130	COMPLETELY DISCHARGED

Approximate state-of-charge condition at different specific gravity levels is measured by hydrometer.

lattice. Two types of plates are then built upon these grids. Positive plates are made by coating the grid with lead peroxide (for you chemistry buffs, it's PbO_2); negative plates use a sponge-lead coating (Pb).

Plates are welded into plate groups and then connected to plate straps. Positive and negative plate groups are interlocked (much like interlacing your fingers) to form a battery cell with alternating positive and negative plates. Between each positive and negative plate is a separator to prevent the unlike plates from touching, causing an internal short.

The plate groups are assembled and placed in the battery case, which is usually made of a hard rubber or polyethylene plastic. Each plate group has its own chamber with the case, forming a reservoir for the electrolyte fluid. When the cell is filled, the electrolyte flows freely between the unlike lead plates, causing a reaction that creates the electrical potential, better known as voltage. Each battery cell is designed to produce 2 volts. By connecting cells in series, batteries can be built to provide 2, 4, 6, 8, 10, 12 or more volts.

The 12-volt battery is most common. Higher voltage batteries have more potential for self-discharge by current leaking to ground, and lower voltage batteries have trouble supplying enough voltage to the vehicle's ignition system while cranking the engine.

Deep Cycle

Deep-cycle batteries make it possible to tailor the battery to the intended use. Motorhomes tend to drain batteries slowly and frequently. But batteries that are designed primarily for starting engines produce a rapid, high-amperage, short-term discharge that starters require. When subjected to the slow, frequent discharge/charge routines (motorhome service), these batteries tend to fail more often than they should as positive-plate material sheds and drops to the bottom of the battery case.

The deep-cycle battery's construction utilizes increased density lead on the cell plates. It is more resistant to breaking down under frequent discharge/charge operation, resulting in an increased lifespan for the battery. For this reason, most deep-cycle batteries are not well suited for all-purpose duty because they are not able to release the high amperage required by starters. The problem becomes particularly noticeable in cold weather, when power required to start an engine at 0°F increases by up to 250 percent.

Maintenance-Free Batteries

Maintenance-free batteries use a different lead alloy on the plates. Instead of a lead-antimony alloy, a lead-calcium alloy is utilized. The calcium reduces battery gassing during charge cycles and, combined with a special battery-cell cap that condenses water and returns it to the cells, the battery requires less frequent or no additions of water.

If you own an older motorhome and have trouble keeping a maintenance-free battery at full charge, the problem may be associated with the voltage output of the charging system. Maintenance-free batteries with lead-calcium plates need higher voltage to bring the battery to charge; calcium increases the resistance to charging.

Many of the older vehicles had voltage regulator settings of between 13.5 and 14.2 volts. To properly charge a maintenance-free battery, voltage needs to be between 13.8 and 14.6. In some cases a change to a later model voltage regulator may be necessary.

Hybrid Batteries

Some batteries are designed to provide enough cranking amps to start engines while providing deep-cycle service for operating appliances. Called hybrids, these batteries are constructed of lead-calcium plates used in maintenance-free batteries and lead-antimony plates used to build deep-cycle versions.

Battery Ratings

Batteries are rated in several different ways, each of which should be scrutinized by the consumer. Since motorhomes generally place a huge demand upon the battery, shop for the best; cutting corners with off-brand, bargain-basement batteries will eventually come back to haunt you.

Cold-Cranking Amps

The cold-cranking amp rating is the number of amps a battery can produce for a 30-second time period at 0°F without the terminal voltage dropping below 7.2 volts. This is a very important number to consider, as it is a good indicator of a battery's performance ability. For motorhome use, look for batteries with a cold-crank amp rating of 500 or above.

Reserve Capacity

This rating, which is specified in minutes, was originally developed to give the consumer an idea of how long a vehicle could run if the charging system failed. For example, a reserve-capacity rating of 120 would indicate that a battery could produce 25 amps for 120 minutes at 80°F before the terminal voltage dropped below 10.2 volts.

In summer, keeping a coach battery in tip-top shape is easy. Just give it regular inspections, don't let corrosion and dirt get a start, keep electrolyte filled to the proper level, and make sure the charging system is performing correctly. By following these simple steps, a motorhome owner can insure his battery will have a long, productive life, resulting in many years of happy traveling.

Maintenance Plus:

Brake Systems

Understanding, inspecting and early servicing can insure safe stopping

Brian Robertson

Even though you may be driving a half-million-dollar luxury coach with every conceivable option, no system on the vehicle is more important than the braking system. Brakes are often taken for granted, as they are used thousands of times with nary a whimper.

But the first time the pedal goes to the floor, you'll gain instant appreciation for that small lever that hangs beneath the dash.

Inspection

As a motorhome owner, the best inspection is to observe how the brakes feel. Strange noises, pedal pulsations, increase or decrease in pedal effort, pulling to one side, fading or grabbing are warning signs that the brake system is subject to failure. A good policy is to inspect the brakes yearly, or every 15,000 to 20,000 miles.

A typical brake inspection includes visual checks of the master cylinder and brake fluid, the power-booster system, brake rotors, brake drums, brake pads and linings, wheel cylinders and calipers, brake hoses and lines, and the parking-brake mechanism. If your motorhome is one with a tag-axle assembly, don't forget it may have brakes, too. A brake inspection must be complete; failure of a single component can cause complete failure of all or part of the braking system.

Backyard inspection of motorhome brakes can be strenuous and time consuming. The process requires loosening 32 tightly torqued lug nuts to wrestle with six clumsy wheel-tire assemblies. But determining possible failure before expensive parts are destroyed is worth the effort.

Master Cylinder

A brake-system inspection should start at the master cylinder, located on the firewall. First, check the exterior of the cylinder for any signs of brake-fluid leakage. External leakage may show up where the cylinder

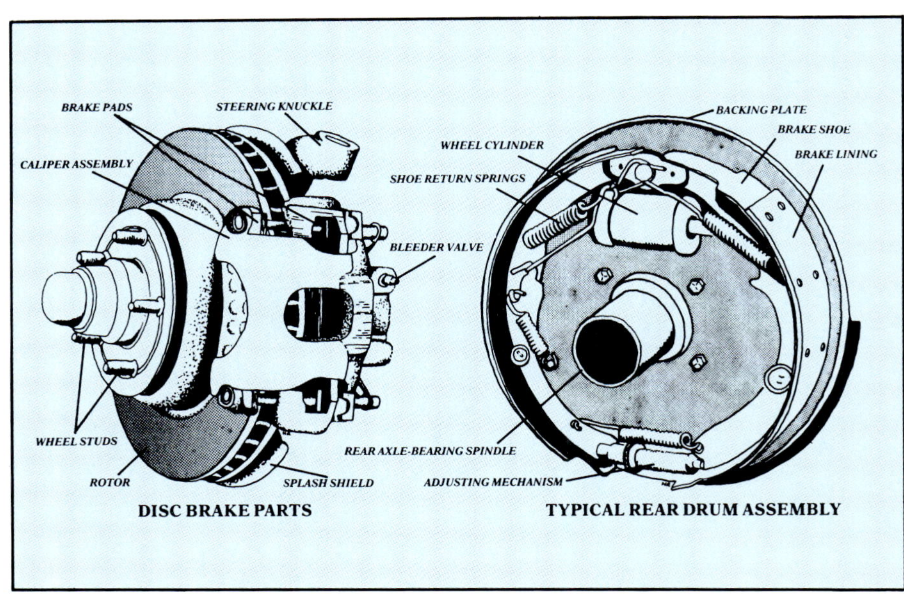

Motorhome chassis are typically equipped with disc brakes up front and either disc or drum brakes in the rear. These drawings have been simplified for clarity, and all parts are not present.

attaches to the brake booster, indicating a defective cylinder piston seal, or near the brake-line fittings, indicating a loose connection or cracked brake line. A defective master-cylinder cover gasket may also cause fluid to leak to the outside.

With the engine running, apply moderate pressure on the brake pedal, holding for about 30 seconds. The pedal should not creep downward. Pedal creep during applied pressure indicates a possible internal master-cylinder leak or possible leakage at a wheel cylinder, caliper piston or brake hose.

Brake Fluid

While inspecting the master cylinder, it's a good idea to check the condition and level of the brake fluid. By removing the master-cylinder cover, both conditions can be checked at the same time.

Brake fluid should be clean and clear. It's somewhat difficult to tell, since the dark-colored cylinder reservoir bottom will cause the fluid to look dark. But by shining a flashlight into the chamber, you should be able to see the bottom. Fluid that is cloudy, brown or rust-colored is probably contaminated and if allowed to remain in the system will shorten the life of all hydraulic components. Dirty fluid should be flushed from the system with a pressure bleeder used by brake repair shops.

Fluid level should be about 1/4 inch below the top of the reservoir. In most cases, a low chamber indicates brake-pad wear. Normally the largest chamber closest to the power booster or rear of the master cylinder is for the disc brakes, and the level of the fluid falls as it fills the caliper piston chamber. Do not top off the low chamber until new pads are installed and the caliper piston is forced back into its bore, displacing extra fluid back to the reservoir.

Frequent additions of brake fluid should not be required unless there is a leak somewhere in the system.

Power Booster

Motorhome chassis have power-booster systems to assist in applying the brakes. The system will be either a vacuum-assist or a hydro-boost system, usual for Class A chassis.

Engine vacuum activates a large diaphragm to help apply pressure to the master cylinder. A vacuum-boost system has a large, round, black

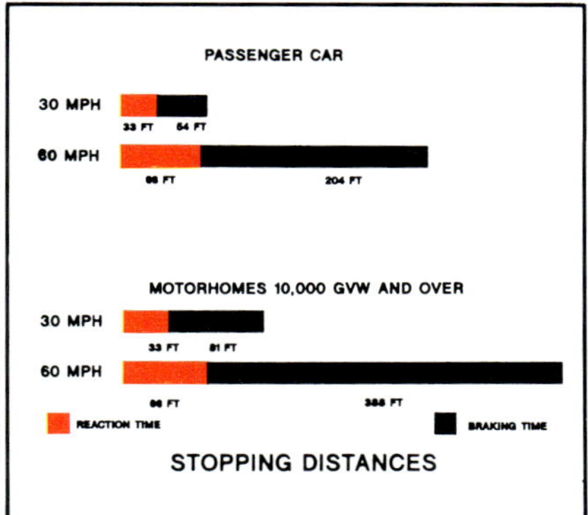

Motorhomes require longer stopping distances than cars; shown are maximum allowable distances by federal laws.

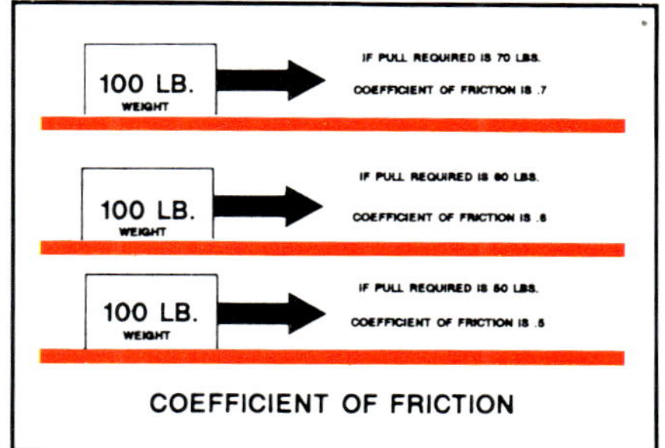

Differences in surface friction will change the coefficient of friction. The coefficient of friction is much higher for a 100-pound weight being pulled over an asphalt surface than a 100-pound weight being pulled over ice.

canister, about 8 inches in diameter, immediately to the rear of the master cylinder. Not a lot of checks can be performed on the canister itself, but vacuum is supplied through a hose connecting to the intake manifold on the engine. Inspect the hose for cracks, and make sure clamps are secure.

Signs of a defective vacuum booster are an increase in braking effort or extremely sensitive brakes that require almost no pedal pressure. In cases where the diaphragm or internal vacuum valve have failed, hissing from under the dash may indicate a vacuum leak is present. Poor engine idle will usually accompany a vacuum leak.

Hydro-boost systems utilize oil pressure from the power-steering pump. The hydro-boost system will have hydraulic oil lines from the power-steering pump to the rear of the master cylinder. Make sure there are no cracks or leaks in the hoses; the power-steering pump reservoir should be filled to the correct level with an approved power-steering fluid.

Check the power-steering pump belt to make sure it is adjusted correctly; a loose belt will cause hard steering and increased brake pedal effort. An increase in steering and brake effort are normal when the engine is at idle and you are making rapid steering motions while braking hard. This is because the pump is being taxed by demands for large volumes of oil at a low pump speed.

Brake Rotors

Because of the open, exposed nature of disc brakes, rotors are easily checked. With the wheels removed from the vehicle, a visual inspection of the rotor's surface can be made. Deep scoring, discolored and burned rotors must be removed and resurfaced. Rotors should be measured with a micrometer to see if they meet the manufacturer's minimum wear thickness standard and to determine if the surfaces are parallel. Specifications should be listed in the service manual.

If the rotors have been surfaced in the past, they may be undersize. Removing too much surface material results in a weakened rotor and reduces the heat absorption and dissipation capacity. Undersized rotors must be replaced.

Rotors with surfaces that are not parallel cause pulsation in the brake pedal. If they meet the minimum thickness requirement, they can be surfaced to correct this problem.

Wheel-bearing adjustment should be checked and rotor runout determined with a dial indicator. Rotor runout or wobble due to uneven wear, distortion, or bad wheel bearings can also cause pulsating pedal and periodic squeaks, rattles and sometimes low brake pedal. Excessive runout may be corrected with resurfacing, but if it is severe, rotor replacement is necessary.

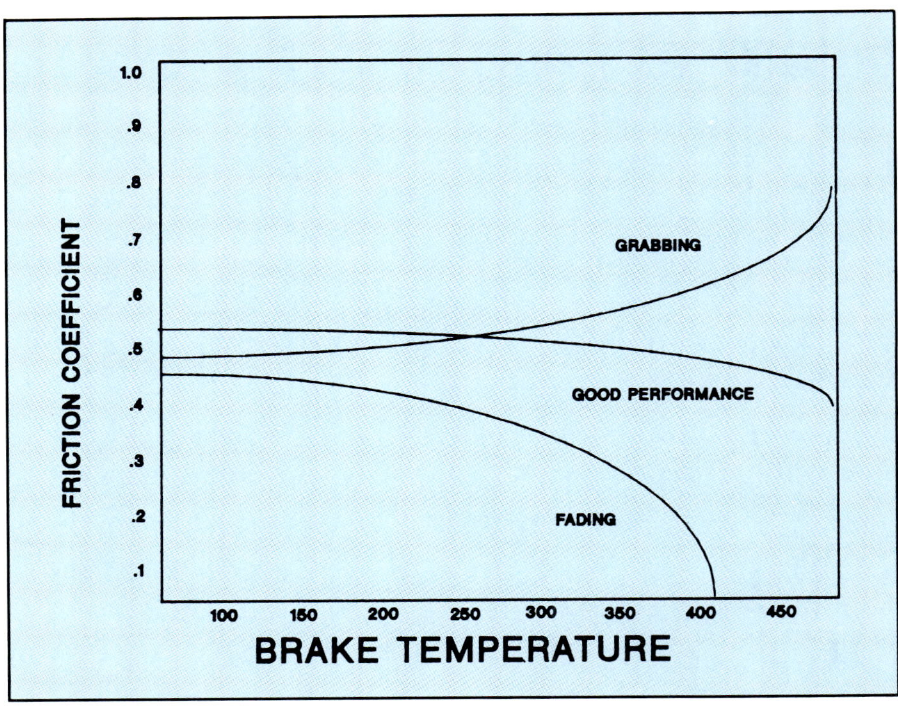

Quality brake linings will maintain an even coefficient of friction over a wide range of temperature variations. Poor quality linings may grab or fade as temperatures between frictional surfaces increase.

Brake Drums

Brake drums are more difficult to inspect than disc rotors. Removal of the tire, wheel and wheel bearings is necessary. In most cases, the drive axles must be removed from the differential and that's not a job for the inexperienced home mechanic. An important pointer: Never press the brake pedal while the drums are removed. Without the drums surrounding the shoes, the hydraulic pressure will cause the wheel cylinders to overtravel and permit the seals to be pushed from the bore.

Drums should be checked for oversize, unlike checking a rotor for undersize. A special brake-drum micrometer is used to determine the size. The manufacturer usually stamps the maximum wear size allowed on the outside rim of the drum. After several surfacings, drums become too thin to maintain their shape under pressure from the brake shoes, and they lose their ability to dissipate heat. Oversize drums must be replaced.

A thorough drum inspection may also find out-of-round drums, bell-mouthed drums, tapered condition, scoring and hard spots. All of these conditions can be repaired by resurfacing if enough material remains so that the drum will not be oversize.

Pads and Linings

While inspecting rotor and drum conditions, the disc pads and drum linings can be checked. For disc pads, manufacturers usually specify a minimum pad thickness. This can be measured while inspecting the rotors.

For the brake shoes on drum brakes, the linings need replacement if the lining thickness is closer to the rivet heads than 1/32 inch or, in the case of bonded linings, at least 1/16 inch of material should remain on the shoe.

Pads and linings should also be checked for contamination from brake fluid, grease and oil. Oil-soaked linings cannot be saved; replace them and the defective seal or seals that caused the leaking condition.

The hard use of brakes will many times cause linings to develop heat

PHOTOS: NANCY ROBERTSON

Top left, ***Grooves can be worn into the drum if the brake shoes are allowed to wear too thin. This requires resurfacing the drums or replacing them if they are badly damaged or oversize.*** **Top right,** ***When brake shoes wear so thin that the rivets make contact with the drum, damage occurs. Routine inspection of the drums and shoes helps avoid damage due to excess wear.*** **Bottom left,** ***The rotor should be inspected periodically to detect abnormal wear. When brake pads wear thin, or foreign objects become lodged between pad and rotor, grooves can be worn in the rotor.*** **Bottom right,** ***The disc-brake pad is easily inspected for cracks, chips, and general wear. Replacment is also a very easy job.***

cracks. These cracks can eventually lead to lining separation and eventually disintegration, perhaps even causing total loss of braking from that wheel.

Wheel Cylinders and Calipers

Wheel cylinders can be visually inspected. The boots can be lifted slightly away from the cylinder to check the bore. A small amount of brake fluid residue is usually present. If fluid drips out from under the boot, it indicates a faulty cylinder-cup seal, which will require rebuilding or replacing.

Calipers are easily checked for seal leaks; a visual indication of fluid will be seen on the disc rotor and caliper if a seal is bad.

Brake Hoses and Lines

If a brake hose or line fails, a sudden drop in hydraulic pressure will render part of the brake system ineffective. Brake-line tubing is made of steel and is susceptable to corrosion and damage from road stones and other debris. Tubing should be checked for dents, rust and cracks. If your motorhome has been driven extensively on salted winter highways or over muddy roads, brake-line corrosion will eventually take its toll.

Flexible rubber brake hoses (to the calipers) are subjected to extreme flexing and possible chafing against metal parts. Hoses should be examined for fatigue cracks and rub marks. Rub marks most commonly occur on the front brakes, since tires and suspension components may touch the hose.

Tag-Axle Brakes

Many larger motorhomes utilize a tag axle to upgrade gross vehicle weight rating (gvwr). Another benefit of the tag axle is that it often adds extra brakes to assist in stopping the rig. Tag-axle brakes are usually a drum/shoe arrangement and are operated either electrically, similar to trailer brakes, or hydraulically, as are the other wheels.

Inspection procedures are similar for the tag axle. If the tag-axle brakes are electric, inspection of the brake magnets, armature and controller is a must. Electric wiring must be scrutinized as carefully as hydraulic lines and hoses. Controller adjustment is critical to proper operation; too much braking force on the tag will result in short brake life and possible skidding of the tag axle's tires. Too light an adjustment will not optimize the ability of the tag to do its job.

Parking Brakes

Parking brakes are usually a mechanical system, completely separate from the hydraulic service brakes. This is to provide a "fail-safe" system that will hold or slow the vehicle, even if total hydraulic failure occurs. On motorhomes, the system usually utilizes the rear brake shoes, applied via a series of levers and cables. Another system found on motorhomes is the driveshaft parking brake, which is simply a mechanical drum-brake assembly mounted on the driveshaft. When applied, it acts to lock rear wheels through the axle differential.

Inspection consists of checking the brake-shoe lining on both types of systems. Further inspection of the cables and levers for rust, wear-through and adjustment completes the parking-brake check. Hand-operated levers usually have a hand adjustment on the end of the lever.

When adjusting the parking brake, free play must remain in the system; otherwise the brakes will drag, rapidly wearing out the shoes and drums. One to 2 inches of free play should be present in a foot pedal, while about 2 inches of free play (measured at the end of the lever) should be apparent in a hand lever before resistance is felt.

Brake Operation Principles

Brakes are amazing, considering less than 100 pounds of pedal pressure can bring a seven-ton motorhome to a standstill from 60 mph in about 6 seconds.

To make this point a bit clearer, consider that a 200-horsepower engine requires about 30 seconds to accelerate the average motorhome to 60 mph. If that same motorhome can be stopped from 60 mph in only 6 seconds, the brakes must absorb five times more energy, or the equivalent of 1,000 horsepower of heat energy. Heat energy is the brake's enemy. In order to continually absorb 1,000 horsepower of braking effort, the brakes must be able to dissipate heat. The brake drums and disc rotors are the dumping grounds, dissipating the heat to the surrounding air.

When engineers design brake components, they must compromise. In order to dissipate all of the heat, an extremely massive system would have to be designed. So braking systems are designed to work at maximum capacity for short intervals, with cooling required between use.

When insufficient cooling time is given, heat builds up to levels where the friction between the shoes and drums or pads and rotors is reduced to nothing, resulting in brake fade.

Brake linings and pads are designed with specific coefficients of friction (see charts). Most linings have a friction coefficient of between .45 and .60. The trick to designing a good-quality lining is to be able to maintain that coefficient of friction, even though the lining temperature changes.

The brake-temperature chart shows how three different linings may perform under elevated temperatures. As temperature increases, linings may rapidly lose their friction coefficient, causing fade. Another type of lining may actually increase its coefficient of friction, causing brakes to grab and lock as temperatures increase. An ideal lining design should hold a relatively stable friction coefficient, whether the brakes are hot or cold.

When you purchase brake linings, go for the expensive, premium grades. These linings will maintain their friction properties over wide temperature ranges while offering a long lifespan.

Remember, next time you're wheeling along the interstate at 60 mph, you need the length of a football field to bring your rig to a halt!

Maintenance Plus:

Play It Cool

A few hours spent servicing a motorhome's cooling system each year can insure against overheating

Brian Robertson

With the heat of summer rapidly approaching, it's vital for motorhomers to pay proper attention to their rigs' cooling systems. Most manufacturers recommend cooling system service every two years, but motorhomes perform under heavy-duty conditions, so it's a good idea to give the entire system a yearly once-over.

Service Stops

Service of your cooling system can be accomplished at home in your driveway. The entire process takes less than one hour, a small amount of time considering that the cost of cooling system repair is expensive.

The first step is to inspect all hoses and clamps for signs of cracking, kinks, softness, looseness, rotting, and corrosion. Defects can be spotted by simply squeezing and bending each hose in the system. Hoses that are hard an inflexible are prone to cracking; cracks in hardened hoses will appear when the hose is bent sharply. Soft spots are an indication of weakness in a hose that may burst unexpectedly under pressure.

A more reliable method of pinpointing defects in the system is by having the system pressure tested. This test simulates operating pressure in the cooling system without the motorhome engine running. The testing device consists of a pressure pump that attaches to the filler neck of the radiator and provides pressure to the system. While simulating operating pressure, the hoses, connections and fittings can be scrutinized for signs of coolant leakage. This same tester is used to check that the radiator cap will hold the proper pressure. A radiator cap that fails to hold pressure effectively lowers the boiling point of the coolant (see chart).

The next inspection step is to check the engine's drive belts. Although modern belts are stronger and last longer, neglect will eventually result

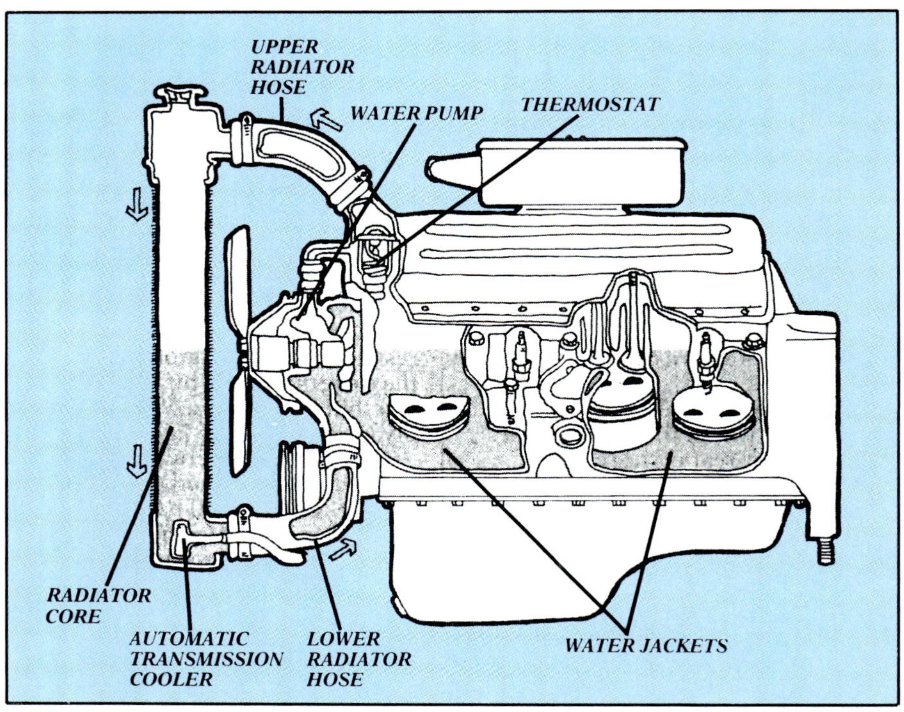

Cross section of typical engine cooling system. Coolant flows into engine through lower radiator hose, transfers heat to radiator via upper radiator hose. Airflow through radiator reduces coolant temperature prior to its return to engine block.

in failure. Belts should show no signs of weathering or cracking. Internal defects are impossible to detect; replace them if they are more than four or five years old, or have seen more than 50,000 miles of service. Carry your old belts as emergency spares. If you ever need a fan belt in a remote town on a sizzling summer day, that old belt can come in mighty handy.

Belt tension is important. There are several belt-tension gauges on the market, but the old thumb deflection method works. There should be about a ½-inch belt deflection while pressing with your thumb. Belt tension that is too light causes slippage, vibration, and short belt life. When the tension is too tight, belt fiber breakage is possible, and bearing life in the rotating accessories on the engine is reduced.

Next, check the radiator core. There should be no signs of leakage or corrosion. Corrosion on a radiator core is indicated by a greenish tint as the copper corrodes, usually indicating a small seepage. The suspect area will feel soft to the touch, and pieces of the radiator fins may crumble. If you suspect that the core is near failing, have a radiator shop check it out. A radiator core for a motorhome can cost more than $400, but you should never have to replace it if proper care is taken. If you neglect the core, have your wallet ready.

Preventive maintenance of the core consists of keeping the radiator fins clean and free from dirt, bugs, and road debris. Dirt lodged in the fins absorbs moisture, causing corrosion. Once a year, force wash the core from the fan side with a garden hose and nozzle or blow it clean with compressed air. If water is used to clean the core, drive the vehicle a few miles to facilitate drying. Installation of a bug screen in front of the radiator goes a long way toward keeping the core clean. Screens can be purchased commercially, or you can make your own from a piece of fiberglass window screen, found at any hardware store.

The cooling system should be drained, backflushed and replenished with a 50% concentration of ethylene-glycol coolant and water every year. An inexpensive backflush device, which uses a garden hose, can

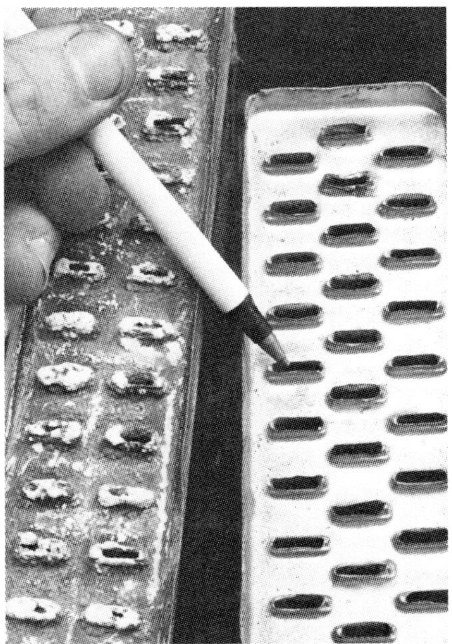

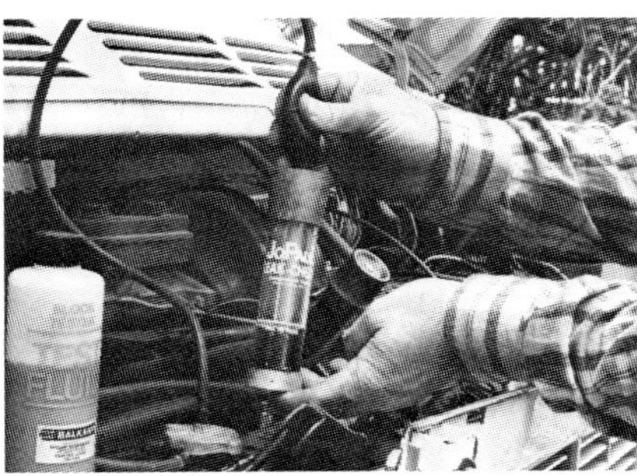

Far left, ***When the radiator core becomes clogged with residue, cooling capacity is greatly reduced.*** **Top,** ***Pressure testing the cooling system and the radiator cap is performed with a manual pressure pump that raises the system to operating pressure.*** **Bottom,** ***Checking for exhaust gas leaks in the cooling system of an engine that overheats can be performed with simple test equipment and gas-sensitive fluid.***

be purchased at auto-supply stores and installed on the engine-to-heater-core hose in a matter of minutes, using only a knife and screwdriver.

With the backflush accessory installed, attach a garden hose, remove the radiator cap, open the heater valve to the full *on* or *hot* position, and turn on the hose. This will force clean water through the top of the engine, into the bottom of the radiator and out the radiator-cap opening. Let the system flush for about five minutes or until the water runs completely clear. If your vehicle has a vacuum-controlled heater valve, the engine must be running with the heat control set on *hot* to open the valve.

After the flushing is complete, turn off the water, remove the garden hose, and drain the system. Open the drain petcock on the bottom of the radiator and, if necessary, remove the lower radiator hose to get as much of the water out as you can. Unless your engine is equipped with block plugs, it is impossible to get all of the water out of the system. However, you only need to get half the water out. Flushing is a little messy, but well worth the inconvenience to remove rust and scale that can do permanent damage.

Check the owner's manual for the cooling system's capacity. The capacity is important because it will determine the amount of ethylene glycol coolant to be added. Depending upon where you live, freeze protection requirements may differ. Most vehicle manufacturers recommend a solution of 50% ethylene glycol and 50% water. This mixture will provide freeze protection −34°F, will increase the boiling point, and will guard against corrosion.

With all the drains closed and radiator hoses connected, fill the system first with antifreeze coolant. Add enough coolant to provide a 50/50 mix based on manufacturer's stated capacity; then fill with water. Run the engine for a few minutes with the heater control on *hot*, and check the radiator level. If the level drops, add water to bring the system to the top. If your motorhome has a closed coolant-recovery system, the level of the coolant/water should be checked in the reservoir after the engine has been at operating temperature and then fully cooled. Fill the reservoir to the "cold fill" mark. This will account for the expansion and contraction of the coolant and insure that all the air is removed from the cooling system.

A handy item is an inexpensive antifreeze hydrometer. These can be found in most parts stores and usually cost less than $5. The hydrometer

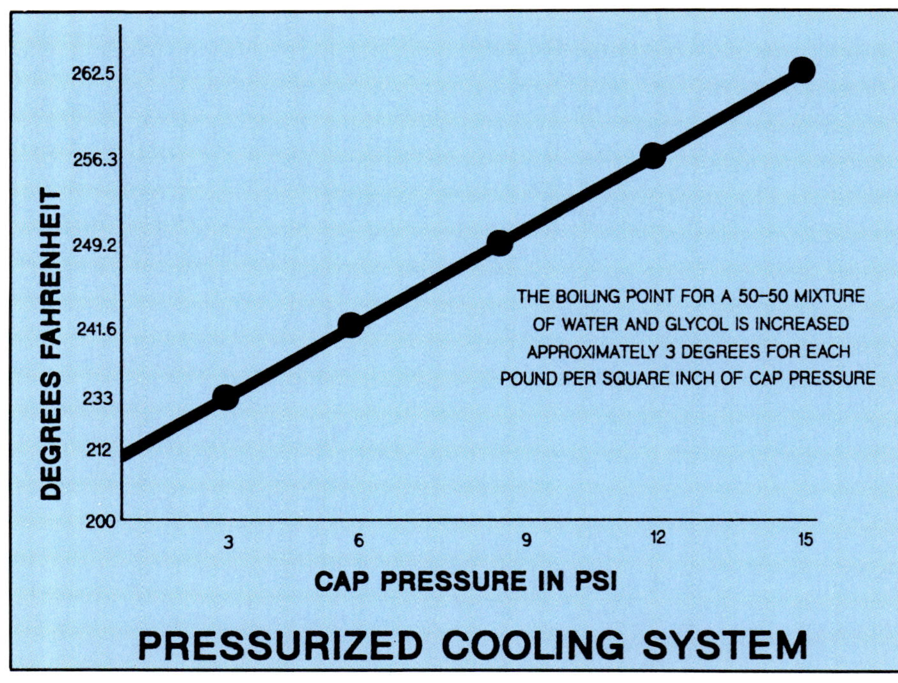

The boiling point of coolant is determined by pressure and the proportion of antifreeze mixed with water.

is used to draw coolant/water from the radiator. The number of small colored balls that float in the glass tube indicates the freezing point.

Proper Operating Temperature

For maximum efficiency, engines are designed to run at a temperature as high as possible without overheating and expelling coolant. Typically, today's motorhome engines are equipped with thermostats to keep the temperature between 190°F and 200°F. Thermostats are commonly the culprit in engine-heating problems and can be easily tested in a pan of water over a stove, using an accurate thermometer (a candy thermometer works well). To do so, hang the thermostat by a wire in the pan of water, so that the thermostat does not touch the metal pan. As the water heats, note the temperature at which the thermostat starts to open. The opening should begin at 10 to 15 degrees less than the thermostat's rating. The thermostat should be nearly full open by the time the rated temperature is reached and fully open 10 degrees above the rating. Removing the thermostat is not a recommended procedure for curing overheating problems.

Overheating

The problem of engine overheating is sometimes mysterious, stumping the best mechanics. Careful evaluation of each system component will yield the best results when diagnosing overheating.

There are several procedures for diagnosing cooling-system problems. The radiator should be closely examined for any internal corrosion buildup (retards heat transfer). The exterior of the radiator should be clean, have an unrestricted airflow, and the fins should be undamaged. The fan/water-pump drive belt must be adjusted so that slippage will not occur. Temperature-controlled clutch fans should be checked for proper engagement temperature. Usually the fan will engage when engine temperature reaches 220°. When it does engage, it creates a loud roar from the engine compartment. Radiator shrouds, which improve air velocity through the core, should be fitted correctly and positioned so the fan blade's plane of rotation is about ½ inch into the shroud opening.

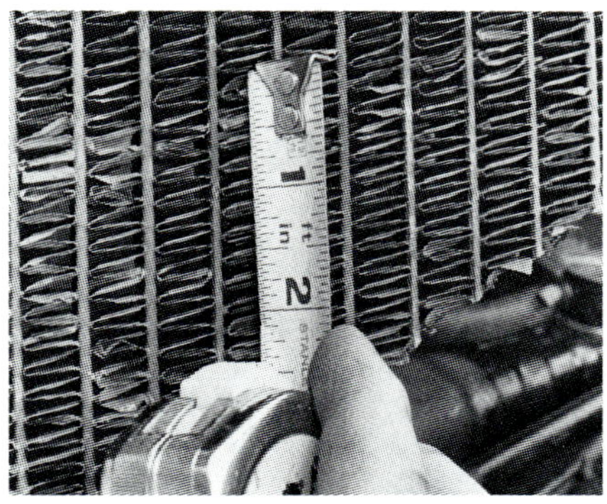

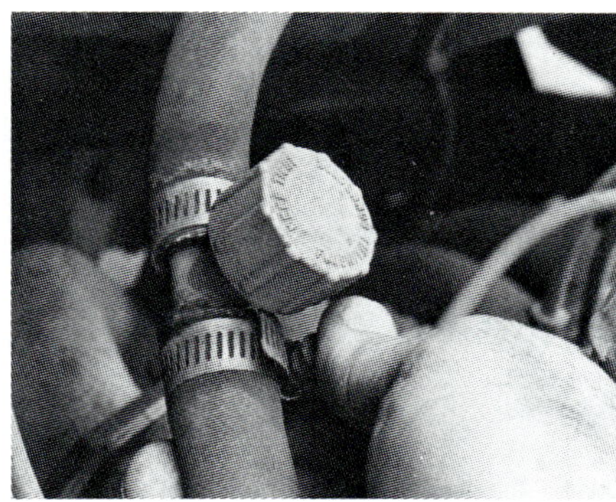

Left, *Heat transfer from coolant to the atmosphere is directly related to radiator size and number of cooling fins per inch.* Right, *Cleaning the cooling system is easy after a back-flush device has been installed in the heater hose. The garden hose connection can be installed in minutes with only a knife and screwdriver.*

Hoses need to be checked for kinks or signs of collapsing. Lower radiator hoses should be fitted internally with a wound coil spring to prevent collapsing and creating a coolant restriction. The engine's water jackets must be clean and free of heat transfer-retarding scale and rust. Water-pump impellers are subject to corrosion damage, which reduces their pumping efficiency. Usually, though, water pumps work fine unless they start to leak, indicating a need for replacement.

Combustion leaks from blown head gaskets or cracked valve seats cause persistent overheating by allowing high-temperature exhaust gases to directly enter the cooling system, raising the coolant/water temperature and overpressurizing the system. A chemical combustion leak test is used to detect and isolate the problem area. A combustion leak test should only be performed on an engine that has been purged of coolant and refilled with water and operated for at least two days.

How the Cooling System Works

Only part of the heat produced by the burning of fuel is used for power production in an internal combustion engine. At 3,000 rpm, approximately 30 percent of the total heat produced goes to propelling your motorhome. About 20 percent of the total heat produced is removed by the cooling system, 45 percent goes out the exhaust pipe, and 10 percent is lost to friction (see chart).

Heat is transferred from the engine in three ways. One method is called convection, which is movement of a mass of air of any given temperature from one place to another. An example is an engine fan moving a mass of heat-carrying air off a motorhome's radiator. Another heat-transfer method is called conduction. This is movement of heat through a solid object due to molecular activity. An example of conduction is the heat of burning fuel in the combustion chamber conducting through the cylinder head and walls to the water in the surrounding water jacket. The third heat-transfer method is radiation, in which heat moves away from an object in the form of rays. Even though a motorhome engine has been shut off and no air circulation exists, heat will radiate when you lift the engine cover.

The System in Action

When an engine is started, a belt-driven water pump draws water from the bottom of the radiator and forces it through the cylinder block and heads. If the engine is cold, the water flows through a small restriction or bypass (thermostat) and is simply recirculated through the engine, skipping the radiator. This allows rapid warming for better performance and longer engine life.

As the engine warms up, a temperature-sensitive thermostat opens, allowing full water circulation to the radiator, where heat is conducted from the hot water to the radiator tubes and fins, and a fan convects the heat from the radiator. This process occurs constantly as the engine is operating. If anything interferes with conduction, convection, or radiation, overheating results. Scale and corrosion buildup on the inside of the engine or radiator will block heat conduction and trap heat within the system. A clean system is an efficient system.

Radiator size is an important factor in the amount of heat that can be removed from an engine. Four factors determine the radiator's effectiveness: core thickness, core width, core height, and number of fins per inch between the tubes.

Core thickness can be increased by adding rows of coolant-carrying tubes to the radiator. This increases the internal surface area for the coolant to conduct heat. Adding width and height may increase the number of tubes, but it mainly adds surface area for air to pass, removing heat by convection. The greater the number of fins per inch between the tubes, the greater the surface area for air to contact, multiplying the amount of fin-to-tube area for increased conduction of heat.

The chart indicates via the lower graph line that a radiator measures 1.25 inches thick, 16.5 inches wide, and 17.5 inches high. By adding 6 inches to the height, as shown in the middle graph line, the capacity to remove heat is increased about 3,000 BTU. But adding only 3/4 inch to the thickness of the core, as shown by the upper graph line, we can get just as large a capacity increase. Many stock factory radiators have only a two-row core. The heat-removal capacity can be greatly increased by replacing a factory core with a four-row unit.

Pressurization of the system is used to increase the boiling point of the coolant. For every 1 pound per square inch (psi) of pressurization, the boiling point is raised by 2½°F. Never replace a cap with one rated higher than your system was designed to use. It will certainly raise the boiling point, but perhaps at the expense of bursting vital system components. The chart shows that a 15-psi cap results in a water-only boiling point of 250°. A mixture of 50/50 ethylene glycol and water increases the boiling point to about 262°.

So there you have it: Proper cooling-system maintenance prevents untimely overheating while increasing the performance and longevity of your motorhome's engine. Preventive maintenance is the best medicine.

Have a cool, cool summer!

Special:

THE CONSTITUTION

Celebrating the Constitution

Barbara Leonard

We, the people of the United States, in order to form a more perfect union, establish justice, insure domestic tranquillity, provide for the common defense, promote the general welfare, and secure the blessings of liberty to ourselves and our posterity, do ordain and establish this Constitution for the United States of America.—Preamble to the Constitution.

PHOTO: *PHILADELPHIA INQUIRER*

Festivities across the nation in 1987 commemorated the 200th anniversary of the signing of the Constitution and invited Americans to pay tribute to the cornerstone of their country.

Designated Bicentennial Communities in more than 40 states roll out the red carpets to honor the document that is the oldest written instrument of national government in the world—the Constitution of the United States. This "miracle," formed 200 years ago in Philadelphia, has come to symbolize our freedom and heritage. It is from this legendary contract that most of the democratic nations of the world have shaped their constitutions. Indeed, none precedes ours, and two-thirds of all national constitutions have been created since 1970!

The Constitutional Bicentennial, which culminated in Philadelphia on September 17, 1987, afforded Americans a great opportunity to reacquaint themselves with this country's origins, the roots of democracy and the system of government that has attracted to our shores tens of millions of people seeking freedom and justice.

RVers, in particular, had a golden opportunity to join in celebrations from coast to coast as they enjoyed their mobile life-style. Everyone was

Re-creation of the signing of the Declaration of Independence is viewed by visitors at historic Independence Hall in Philadelphia, where the actual event occurred. The bespectacled figure in the center represents Benjamin Franklin, a Philadelphia resident who played a key role in the new nation's beginnings.

PHOTO: ALBERT MOLDVAY/PSI

invited to participate in, not merely watch, this moment in history. Unlike other recent celebrations, which included spectacular fireworks and fanfare viewed from afar, the Constitution commemoration urged personal involvement. From the Boy Scouts of America to the American Association of Retired Persons, groups joined the fanfare across the country.

Among the more notable celebrations across the country that RVers attended were those in San Diego, the first city recognized as a Designated Bicentennial Community. This Southern California city featured a commemorative ball and a parade of ships. Maryland put on a four-day celebration of the Annapolis Convention; Illinois had a re-enactment of the signing of the Constitution at its state capitol in Springfield; New Hampshire offered a traveling exhibit on state development; and Delaware restored John Dickinson's plantation and featured a film on the statesman's life.

One of the most colorful and exciting places to celebrate the Constitution was at Walt Disney World in Orlando, Florida. Throughout 1987 the Magic Kingdom and Epcot Center invited visitors to enjoy an all-American marching band, to view artifacts in the American Adventure showcase and to see an animated history of the country in the American Theatre.

And, of course, our nation's capital observed and participated in the festivities in a grand manner. Washington, D.C., offered special museum displays dedicated to educating the American public, including the original Constitution, Declaration of Independence and Bill of Rights. The display, titled "The American Experiment: Creating the Constitution," appeared in the National Archives and will run through 1989. The Archives honored the actual anniversary of the signing of the Constitution with an 87-hour vigil September 13–17, during which time the building was open 24 hours a day for the public to view the original documents. A military honor guard stood watch and guests signed a register.

The focal point of the celebration, however, was the City of Brotherly Love, where the largest parade in the history of the United States took

ILLUSTRATION: TOM O'MARY

ILLUSTRATION: TOM O'MARY

PHOTO: DENNIS A. MOOK

PHOTO: COURTESY DELAWARE STATE TRAVEL SERVICE

Left, *In Portsmouth, Virginia, a day-long Declaration Celebration is held every July 4; on the steps of the 1846 courthouse in the Olde Towne area, an actor portraying Thomas Jefferson reads the Declaration of Independence to the assembled citizens of the town, founded in 1752.* Right, *At many of the re-enactments, participants wear authentic 1700s dress, plus powdered wigs such as this one.*

place on September 17, 1987, Constitution Day. Philadelphia's year-long celebration, officially titled "We the People 200," included the commemoration of the convening of the Constitutional Convention, a Freedom Festival, Maritime America, fife-and-drum parades, musical performances of *Four Little Pages* and an appearance of the Congress of the United States, meeting here for the first time since 1800. Millions of people visited Independence Hall, the Liberty Bell and other historic sites within America's Most Historic Square Mile during the year, but on Constitution Day the city took on a special international overtone, as representatives from 140 countries participated in the national commemoration of the actual signing of the Constitution.

The Grand Federal Procession began from four points within the city and culminated at the Liberty Bell. Floats re-created designs of the first Federal Procession held after the ratification in 1787, and, the day ended with appearances by various executive, legislative, and judicial leaders, representing the branches of the government created by the Constitution.

Philadelphia held one of the grandest and most memorable celebrations the country has ever witnessed.

Join us in celebrating the Constitution on the following pages, where you will find articles on Philadelphia, our first capital, and Delaware, our first state.

Philadelphia

The indomitable spirit of our nation is proudly showcased and celebrated in the City of Brotherly Love

Robert J. Smith

PHOTO: NPS/ROBERT FREAR

During the summer of 1787, 55 delegates from 12 states met in the State House in Philadelphia for a "Grand Convention." For four hot, steamy months they listened, discussed, debated deliberated and compromised before inventing a unique system of government based on fundamental law, a revolutionary document in which the people granted powers to government instead of the other way around; a charter of freedom that has stood for 200 years; the most successful blueprint for popular sovereignty in human history. They had achieved what George Washington, one of the delegates, described as "little short of a miracle"—the Constitution of the United States of America.

The movers and shakers behind this monumental achievement met and worked where much of our nation's formulative history was made, an area now called the Independence National Historical Park, which is often described as "America's most historic square mile."

Located on 42 acres in the center of Pennsylvania's City of Brotherly Love, the park includes 40 buildings dating from before or shortly after 1800. Touring the park is akin to walking through the pages of a living history book. The aura of greatness hovers over the mellowed bricks of Independence Hall and associated structures. It's fitting that this park was the center of the Constitution's great bicentennial gala.

PHOTO: MICHELE BURGESS

In Philadelphia's Independence Hall (this page), the Liberty Bell (facing page) is on display. The symbol of America's freedom carried the inscription: "Proclaim Liberty throughout all the Land unto all the Inhabitants Thereof." It first rang to announce the Declaration of Independence in July, 1776, and cracked in 1835, tolling for Supreme Court Justice John Marshall's funeral.

Right, ***Carriage tours on Chestnut Street are another means for visitors to experience the flavor of the eighteenth century.*** **Below,** ***The clock on the west wing of Independence Hall features an unusual face.***

PHOTO: PAUL HURD

PHOTO: PAUL HURD

We found the best way to visit the numerous attractions is to park your vehicle in the parking garage on 2nd Street between Walnut and Chestnut, about a block away. Here you can view a superb film titled *Independence* and pick up information, books, maps and tickets. Most of the park's attractions are free but a couple require admission tickets, which you can pick up here.

Since the earlier the visit, the shorter the wait, we hurried over to the Liberty Bell Pavilion to view that symbol of freedom. The bell is in a glass-enclosed structure where it can be viewed at any hour, but to get inside and close up, one must join a ranger-escorted tour. Ordered for the General Assembly of Pennsylvania, the great bell's inscription reads, "Proclaim Liberty throughout all the Land unto all the Inhabitants Thereof" (Lev. 25:10). It first rang to proclaim the Declaration of Independence in July, 1776, and it cracked in 1835 when tolling for the funeral of the renowned Supreme Court Chief Justice John Marshall. To us, viewing this symbol was almost a religious experience, and touching it was one of the highlights of our visit.

Our next stop was Independence Hall, where admission is also by ranger-guided tour. This brick Georgian building, constructed between 1732 and 1756, served as Pennsylvania's statehouse. In this hallowed hall some of the most important events of our nation's early history took place. The assembly room, known as the "Signing Room," was the site of the Second Continental Congress in 1775, where the Declaration of Independence was adopted in 1776, the Articles of Confederation were ratified in 1781, and the Constitution was framed in 1787. Look for the chairman's chair, located in the upper center of the room. Occupied by George Washington, its high back bears a half sun, which Benjamin Franklin declared to be a rising sun, symbolic of the success of the new

PHOTO: ROBERT J. SMITH

PHOTO: ROBERT J. SMITH

Top, ***Campgrounds in the area boast magnificent natural settings, especially beautiful groves of old trees like these, which are at their best in late summer and early fall.*** **Bottom,** ***Walking in the 42-acre Independence National Historical Park is a peak patriotic adventure. Its 40 buildings, all dated prior to 1800, seem to echo with the ghosts of the nation's founding fathers.***

republic. The chair and the silver inkstand are originals. The inkstand was used for both the signing of the Declaration of Independence and the Constitution. Other furnishings are authentic recreations.

The Supreme Court Chamber of Pennsylvania is another great room in the statehouse. Even here, the zesty Colonial psyche was unrestrained. Trials were a public attraction, with visitors coming and going at will. Spectators often hissed and booed and, on occasion, threw things at the helpless defendant in the dock.

Upstairs, a 100-foot-long room was the largest room in the colonies. Here many delegates worked to frame the Constitution. The debates and arguments, which took place in strict secrecy, were often heated. The only record of what happened behind these doors comes from James Madison's daily notes. Unpublished for more than 40 years, they are among the most important manuscript records of American history.

Flanking Independence Hall are the Old City Hall and Congress Hall. Congress Hall was the meeting place of the U.S. Congress from 1790 to 1800, the year the offices of the federal government were moved to Washington, D.C.

The bicentennial celebration's premier exhibit, titled "Miracle at Philadelphia," was located in the Second Bank of the United States building. Here you met the delegates face to face, read James Madison's secret notes, and the personal letters of national leaders, heard the sound of debates respoken saw the Constitution as it evolved through its original handwritten drafts to its final form, and signed the completed Constitution yourself! We signed with a gold pen, and it was quite a thrill.

Luncheon at the City Tavern is an event. This gracious tavern, recreated to appear as it did 200 years ago, is one that John Adams called "the most genteel in America." When completed in 1773, it was one of the most elegant buildings in Philadelphia, which was the most cosmopolitan city in the British Colonies. We ordered luncheon from an excellent menu and were served by waiters and waitresses wearing appropriate Colonial costumes.

Carpenters' Hall, where the First Continental Congress met during the autumn of 1774, is a short stroll from City Tavern. This body decided how the Colonies should meet the British threats to their freedom. It united the Colonies from Massachusetts to the Carolinas behind a policy of resistance. In one corner of the fully restored hall, you can see a table,

Almost everywhere in Philadelphia are reminders that the legends taught in school are based on facts about quite exceptional people who inhabited these streets 200 years ago.

chairs, papers and inkstand such as those the delegates used. Incidentally, each delegate had to bring his own chair. This hall, the meeting place of the Carpenters' Company of Philadelphia, has one of the most interesting histories of any building in the city. Its tenants were unusual and varied. You might say it became the first Pentagon when Secretary of War Henry Knox rented the ground floor in 1790. Another of its tenants, the Bank of Pennsylvania, was the victim of America's first great bank robbery, a heist that netted its perpetrators a cool $160,000 in coins and banknotes. Its owner, the Carpenters Company, is the oldest builders' organization in the United States.

PHOTO: COURTESY OF *PHILADELPHIA INQUIRER*

Our next stop was Christ Church, a classic example of Georgian Colonial architecture. Organized in 1695 and completed in 1744, it is regarded as the most important church of Colonial America. Among the notables that worshipped here were Washington, Franklin and Adams. Its resonant bells, cast by the same foundry that made the Liberty Bell, joined in tolling the Declaration of Independence. They are still rung every day.

We found the Betsy Ross House on Arch Street a jewel. This restored 2½-story Colonial house is where Ross convinced George Washington and the flag committee that a five-pointed star was appropriated for our flag. Although it conflicted with her Quaker beliefs, Ross was a patriot. She made flags for the Pennsylvania Navy and musket balls for the Continental Army. We enjoyed climbing about the narrow stairways and viewing the excellent sets that depict life in the house. They are viewed through glass windows. Some of the furnishings belonged to Ross. The house is owned and maintained by the city of Philadelphia; admission is free.

Philadelphia, the City of Brotherly Love, was founded as a Quaker colony by William Penn in 1681. By 1774 it was second only to London as the largest English-speaking city in the world. In addition to the Independence National Historical Park, the city and its environs are crammed with historic buildings. We found one of the best ways to view these attractions was from the Fairmount Park Trolley Bus. For only $2, we enjoyed a fabulous tour that included cultural attractions and many historic mansions. A guide kept up a flow of interesting and factual commentary. This tour begins and ends at the National Park Visitors Center, and one ticket allows you to get on and off at designated stops.

Most park buildings are open from 9 A.M. to 5 P.M. daily, but they are closed on Christmas and New Year's Day. For more information, write the Superintendent, 313 Walnut Street, Philadelphia, Pennsylvania 19106. The city's streets are straight but narrow, and usually clogged with traffic, so it's a good idea to avoid driving RVs downtown, especially during rush hours.

There are several RV parks in the vicinity of Philadelphia. Some operate van tours to the city. Check the *1989 Trailer Life Campground & RV Services Directory* for listings.

The 200th anniversary of the U.S. Constitution was celebrated around the world, but the best place to relive the glory of the nation's beginnings was in America's Most Historic Square Mile. It gave new meaning to the words, "We the People. . . .

Valley Forge

Preserved are the mementos of a young army that sacrificed much to gain the independence of a nation

Robert J. and Geraldine R. Smith

Valley Forge, the icy crucible where the American Revolution withstood its greatest test, is located in the gentle, rolling hill country of southeastern Pennsylvania. Here the Continental Army waged an epic battle against an enemy that was not mortal, but a savage armada whose ammunition was typhus, typhoid, dysentery and pneumonia. These natural forces, allied with the gut-wrenching hunger and biting cold, felled one of every six men who camped here during the winter of 1777–1778.

George Washington led his poorly fed, ill-equipped army into Valley Forge on December 19, 1777. A light snow already covered the ground, and frigid winds searched ragged clothing with icy fingers as the 12,000 Continentals prepared for the encampment. Defense lines were planned, and the construction of 2,000 huts was started. Within days the Schuylkill River, along the camp's northern boundary, was frozen solid, and snow was six inches deep. The ordeal had begun.

Valley Forge, 18 miles northwest of Philadelphia, had been selected for the encampment because the area was close enough to the British, ensconced in Philadelphia, to keep their foraging parties from the interior of Pennsylvania, yet distant enough to preclude a surprise attack. Its high ground made it easily defensible, and it was thought that the fecund farmlands of the area would provide a steady source of supplies. The latter proved untrue. At best the supplies of meat and bread were meager; often the troops subsisted on "firecake," a tasteless mixture of flour and water.

Other supplies were equally short. At times the Continental Army resembled a rabble or horde of beggars. Long marches had destroyed shoes and cloth wrappings had to substitute; tattered clothing was more fitting for scarecrows than soldiers; blankets were scarce or nonexistent.

The animals suffered with the men. General Knox, Washington's chief of artillery, wrote that hundreds of the horses starved to death.

Although the Congress tried, they were unable to persuade the states to provide more than they already had. At Valley Forge suffering became the standard, not the exception. A despairing Washington wrote, ". . . unless some great and capital change suddenly takes place . . . this

Army must inevitably . . . starve, dissolve or disperse, in order to obtain subsistance in the best manner they can."

Supply was just one of the many problems. Upgrading the Continental Army's military efficiency, morale and discipline was vital to its existence. From its inception the army had been handicapped by a lack of uniform instruction. Coordinating battle movements for units trained with such a wide variety of field manuals was difficult, nigh impossible. The task of remedying the latter fell to Baron Friedrich von Steuben, a Prussian aristocrat and former aide to Frederick the Great.

PHOTO: ROBERT J. SMITH

The great National Memorial Arch commemorates the "patience and fidelity" of the soldiers who suffered in Valley Forge.

Von Steuben arrived at Valley Forge from France on February 23, 1778, with a letter of introduction from Benjamin Franklin. Washington, sensing the ability of the Prussian, assigned him the duties of acting inspector general with the task of developing and carrying out an effective training program.

The task was enormous. No standard American manual existed, morale was low, and von Steuben spoke little English. Undaunted, the Prussian wrote his own manual in French and had his aides translate it into English. The translations were quickly copied and passed to the individual regiments, which carried out the prescribed drill the next day.

The agonizing winter passed slowly, but the Army, held together by Washington's inspirational leadership, underwent a dramatic change. The endurance, bravery and sacrifice of the men began to tell. Increasing amounts of supplies and equipment came into camp, and new troops arrived to fill the depleted ranks. Spring found the survivors of the terrible ordeal a strong, dependable, well-trained force, ready and eager to fight the war.

Word of the British retreat from Philadelphia brought this army in pursuit. The results of von Steuben's training were soon apparent as the Continentals successfully engaged British regulars in open field combat at Monmouth, New Jersey. Although the war would last for five more years, the ordeal at Valley Forge assured its victory—American independence would live.

Nearly 10 years later that independence would be cemented in place by the signing of the Constitution of the United States on September 17, 1787, in nearby Philadelphia.

The Valley Forge National Historical Park is located at the junction of State Highways 23 and 363. There is no admission fee for the park or the audio-visual programs that furnish background material on the happenings here. In addition, at the visitors center you can see a number of interesting exhibits that display the artifacts of the day, as well as an excellent collection of arms of the period. One of the more unusual exhibits here is Washington's tent. The tent, marquee styled, was passed on to his adopted son, Parke Custis, who in turn passed it one to his daughter Mary, who became the wife of Robert E. Lee. The visitors center is the place to pick up informative, illustrated maps.

On our tour we passed extensive remains and reconstructions of major fortifications and earthworks. The route includes the area where General Peter Muhlenberg's Brigade manned the outer lines of defense. As you look into the re-created huts you soon realize just how precarious was the army's position here during the winter months. The poorly heated and ventilated huts were a major cause of disease. At one point, supply shortages and disease caused nearly 4,000 men to be listed as unfit for duty.

The great National Memorial Arch, dedicated in 1917, commemorates the "patience and fidelity" of the Valley Forge veterans.

The focal point of Valley Forge activities was the Isaac Potts House, where Washington's headquarters were located. We prowled through the building and climbed a narrow stairway to the second floor bedroom where Washington had slept. A guide, dressed as an aide, answered questions about the house.

Nearby are the huts of the Commander's Guard. This is a lovely area along the banks of the Schuylkill River. Its pastoral beauty gives no hint of the trying times of those bygone days.

The tour route covers both the inner and outer lines of defense. You can quickly see how the emplaced cannon could command the approaches.

A long line of cannon marks the Artillery Park. Here, under the command of Brigadier General Henry Knox, the guns were stored and repaired, and gun crews were trained.

We were impressed with the massive statue of von Steuben that overlooks the Grand Parade ground. It was here, on the only level surface in the encampment big enough for massed brigades to maneuver, that von Steuben sent the troops back and forth in simulated battle. Here he trained the men in the use of the bayonet, a weapon that decided the outcome of most eighteenth-century battles.

The privately owned Washington Memorial Chapel and the Valley forge Historical Society Museum are located on the grounds. A small fee is charged.

The park is open daily from 8:30 A.M. to 5 or 6 P.M., depending on the time of year. It is closed Christmas Day. For more information write: Superintendent, Valley Forge National Historical Park, Valley Forge, Pennsylvania 19481.

The tour route accommodates RVs, but there is no camping in the park. There are a number of RV parks in the general area. Consult the *1989 Trailer Life Campground & RV Services Directory* for listings.

Valley Forge is one of those places that bring deep patriotic feelings to the surface. Even though we usually visit when the hills are green and the weather sunny, there is something about the place that speaks of heroism and sacrifice above and beyond the call of duty. It was truly a frigid crucible in which liberty was cast.

The First State

Delaware's rich cultural heritage echoes the voices of our nation's founders

Bill and Bert Schill

Delaware, nicknamed the First State because it was the first to ratify the new U.S. Constitution may be small in size but it's far from small when it comes to history. Within its slight perimeter, RVers will find a bonanza of historical and recreational attractions.

In 1638, three ships carried Swedish settlers up the Delaware River to a tributary they named Christina, in their queen's honor. They built a fort and permanent settlement on the riverfront, which became the state's largest city, Wilmington.

To mark the 300th anniversary of the Swedish settlement in America, a monument representing the *Kalmar Nyckel,* the settlers' flagship, was presented to Delaware by the people of Sweden and it now stands in a park at the foot of Seventh Street. There is also a log cabin on the grounds typical of the housing in which the early pioneers lived. The park is closed Monday and holidays and is open Tuesday through Saturday, 10 A.M. to 4:30 P.M.; Sundays, 1:30 to 4:30 P.M.

And in the riverfront area, the U.S. Coast Guard cutter *Mohawk* is berthed at the foot of King Street on the Christina River, as a memorial to the men who fought with her in the North Atlantic.

The *Lady Christina,* a cruise ship, is also docked at the foot of King Street near the Pennsylvania railroad. Lunch, dinner, sightseeing and show cruises are available on the Christina and Delaware rivers.

New buildings are constantly emerging to alter Wilmington's cityscape, and as part of the revitalization of downtown, the Market Street pedestrian mall combines the past with the present. Wilmington Square, at 506 Market Street Mall, contains four eighteenth-century houses that were moved to this site for preservation, and in the 800 block of the mall is the beautiful Grand Opera House, an excellent example of 1871 cast-iron architecture. Edwin Booth, George M. Cohan and Maud Adams were among the headliners who performed in this imposing old theater.

At 512 Market Mall, the Old Town Hall (1798–1800) is now a museum housing memorabilia of the past, children's toys, changing exhibits and restored jail cells. A memorial procession for George Washington originated at this Georgian-style building in 1799, and receptions and dinners were held for the Marquis de Lafayette, President Andrew Jackson,

The New Castle Court House is open to the public all year.

PHOTO: BILL AND BERT SCHILL

ners were held for the Marquis de Lafayette, President Andrew Jackson, General William Henry Harrison and Daniel Webster. In 1851, Henry Clay's body lay in state in the Old Town Hall.

Throughout Wilmington there are many historic properties located in the Delaware Avenue, Market Street, Shipley Run, Eighth Street// Tilton Park Quaker Hill, Coal Spring and Baynard Boulevard districts, each having its own special characteristics dating back to the early 1700s.

The city also offers modern shops and a variety of restaurants—from country kitchen to French cuisine—that will suit any performance. As an added incentive to trying local specialties, the state has no sales tax.

Another attraction to enjoy when visiting Wilmington is a ride on the Wilmington & Western Railroad, a real steam train. Running between Greenville and Mount Cuba, a 9-mile track crisscrosses a creek over wooden trestles and dips through woods and farmlands.

The station is located at the junction of State Highways 2 and 41, at Greenbank, where there is free parking and the largest open-air flea market in Delaware. The train runs on weekends: Saturday from June to September; Sunday from May through October. A special event is featured every Sunday, such as the re-enactment of The Great Train Robbery.

No visit to Delaware can be made without the name du Pont coming into the picture. The epitome of elegance and wealth is captured in the palatial mansion built for Alfred I. and Jessie Ball du Pont in 1909,

Top, *During Old Dover Days, held each May in the state's capital, visitors enjoy a house-and-garden tour with an arts-and-crafts marketplace, Colonial games and a parade. Local participants wear period costumes, adding to the fun.* Below, *Tailgaters gather to enjoy the Point-to-Point steeplechase race at Winterthur. This world-class museum, open year-round, is especially popular during the fall foliage season.*

named Nemours after the du Pont ancestral home in north-central France. North of Wilmington on Rockland Road, Exit 8 off Interstate 95, this 300-acre estate showcases beautiful French-style gardens with marble stairs, statuary, fountains and a Russian gate made for Catherine the Great, Empress of Russia.

The mansion contains 77 rooms filled with fascinating curios collected by the du Ponts on their numerous travels abroad. Many of the walls and central ceilings are embellished with 24-carat-gold designs, and it is breathtaking to stroll through the rooms and gaze on the opulence of English furniture, Persian rugs, original paintings, crystal chandeliers and intricate wall tapestries.

PHOTOS: BILL AND BERT SCHILL

There is also a wonderful collection of antique cars in mint condition, a bowling alley and a game room. While the grandeur is almost overwhelming, there are some homey touches in du Pont's personal trophy collection and a mounted striped bass caught by Jessie du Pont.

Still another du Pont estate is the lovely Winterthur, purchased by Henry Francis du Pont in 1927. Dating back to 1837, this country house was turned into a museum of 196 rooms containing all American-made furniture and antiques. Henry du Pont bought entire rooms from homes along the Eastern Seaboard and had them transported to his home, setting them up in their original state. He then purchased authentic furniture and fixtures to fill the rooms, so they would be preserved as a showcase from an earlier era for visitors to enjoy.

As a collector, du Pont was extremely fond of the American eagle, and a variety in gold and natural wood carvings can be seen throughout the museum.

One of the most spectacular rooms is the Chinese parlor, with hand-painted paper on the walls and two magnificent carved screens. The furniture is in the Chinese Chippendale style.

From six silver tankards crafted by Paul Revere, rare eighteenth-century knife urns on a sideboard, to furniture with claw-and-ball feet, these rooms represent homes in the 13 original states and contain more than 71,000 articles, some of which can only be seen here.

There are 13 varieties of gardens on the more than 900 acres, and the vistas change with every season.

Several events are held on the grounds each year, and one of the most interesting is the Point-to-Point steeplechase held the first Sunday in May. This race draws thousands of spectators, who spread blankets on the grassy knolls and picnic, or park their vehicles and have tailgate parties, while they watch riders guide their beautiful horses over the hill-and-dale race course. To open the event, there is a parade of antique horse-drawn carriages, including a wicker pony cart, gigs, traps, surreys and farm wagons. The drivers of the coaches and their guests dress in the styles prevalent in the early nineteenth century. Following the parade of carriages, there are junior riders in pony competitions, the steeplechase over post-and-rail timber fences and a flat race.

Rounding out the festivities, colorful tents are set up for socializing by the sponsoring corporations, while French, Philadelphia and Chesapeake cuisine is available for anyone who did not bring a picnic lunch.

To really step back into the past, six miles below Wilmington on State Route 9 is the delightfully quiet and colonial town of New Castle. The original cobblestone Market Street runs between Harmony and Delaware streets and leads past the old arsenal, built in 1809, now the New Castle Inn, where delicious food is served.

At the corner of Delaware Street is the Town Hall (built in 1823) with an arch through its center opening into the marketplace that dates back to 1682.

The Old Court House on Delaware Street flies four flags from the balcony: Netherlands, Sweden, Britain and the United States. This was Delaware's colonial capitol, and the State Assembly met here until 1777. The cupola atop the building was the measuring point of a 12-mile radial circle, surveyed by Mason and Dixon, to form Delaware's northern boundary with Pennsylvania.

The four flags denote New Castle's fascinating history. The town, first named Fort Casimir, was founded by the Dutch, under Governor Peter Stuyvesant in 1651 after defeating the Swedes at Wilmington. The Swedes, in turn, recaptured the fort in 1654, then once again, Stuyvesant retook the town. After this sortie, he laid out the streets and the green and the town became New Amstel. This ended the Swedes' expectations of colonizing this area of the New World, since the Dutch now occupied the land from Cape Henlopen in the south of Delaware to what is now New York state, dividing the English colonies to the north and south. King Charles II sent two armed vessels to New Amstel to attack the stockade. The small garrison of Dutch surrendered, and the town was renamed New Castle, becoming the property of Charles' brother, the Duke of York, later King James II.

Under the British, bricks were made, homes built and defenses reinforced, but during the Anglo-Dutch war in 1673, the Dutch again captured the town for Prince William of Orange. The influx of English colonists, however, was too much for the Dutch; they withdrew their claims on New Castle in 1674.

In 1682, William Penn first set foot in Delaware at New Castle, which was included in his land grant consisting of Pennsylvania and the three lower counties of Delaware.

Lord Baltimore, in Maryland, contested these claims, which resulted in bitter bickering and, at times, violence. Finally, in 1704, Delaware was given the three lower counties and its own assembly, which made New Castle the capital.

Many meetings and debates over the Stamp and Navigation Acts were held in the Old Court House, and delegates to the Continental Congress were appointed in 1775; in 1777 the government seat was moved to Dover. Two of the signers of the Declaration of Independence were New Castle residents George Read and Thomas McKean.

The green is just that today, but in 1655 it was an area used for grazing by various barnyard animals. Diagonally across the street is the Cellar, a small but very nice restaurant. This was once the site of the public well, the foundation of which can be seen in the restaurant.

Across Third Street, toward the far end of the green, is the Old Dutch House Museum. This intriguing little brick house is reputed to be the only complete survivor in its original form built prior to 1700 and the oldest brick dwelling in Delaware.

Next door is the old Library Museum, an especially interesting building since it is hexagonal. There are exhibits and a slide presentation available; free admission. Hours are Thursday and Saturday, 11 A.M. to 4 P.M.; Sunday, 1 to 4 P.M.

At the corner of Third and Harmony streets, the Immanuel Church and graveyard draw a lot of interest. Founded in 1689, this was the first Church of England parish in Delaware. Built in 1703, the church burned in 1980, but was rebuilt using the original walls. George Read is buried in the graveyard, and Benjamin Franklin wrote some of the epitaphs on the headstones.

Turning into the Strand toward Delaware Street you'll note the George Read II house. Built by the son of the signer of the Declaration of Independence, this handsome building, in a formal garden setting, has an entrance with a distinctive fanlight under an iron balcony.

The Strand has many interesting homes today, but in its fledgling days it was lined with inns. Adjacent to the busy waterfront, it offered lodging for travelers when packets plied the Delaware River.

New Castle is a small town, but ideal for walking and chatting with friendly people, who are more than willing to talk about their colonial background.

Most campgrounds are seasonal, but the Odessa KOA, 18 miles south of New Castle, is open all year. Located on Blackbird Landing Road, off Route 301, this was a convenient spot to set up our trailer and commute to New Castle and Wilmington.

For further information regarding times, dates of special events and tours, admission fees and brochures, contact: Catherine Wheeler, Director of Tourism Marketing, P.O. Box 1401, 99 Kings Highway, Dover, Delaware 19903; (800) 282-8667 in state; (800) 441-8846 out of state.

With its great wealth of historic preservation, grand manors, cultural institutions and magnificent gardens, it is easily understood why Delaware claims to be "The Small Wonder."

INDEX

Abbeville, Louisiana, 34
Acadia National Park, Maine, 5–10
Acadiana, Louisiana, 35
Address, permanent legal, 112
Ainsworth State Park, Oregon, 74, 75
American Revolution, 181–182
Antifreeze hydrometers, 165–166
Antonito, Colorado, 121, 124
Appalachian Arts and Crafts Festival, 17
Arches National Park, Utah, 65, 66–69, 146
Arizona, quail-hunting in, 131–132
Atherton Creek Campground, Teton National Forest, 142–143
Automatic teller machines (ATMs), 113
Avery Island, Louisiana, 34, 35

Babcock State Park, West Virginia, 16
Baja California, Mexico, 84–96
  Espíritu Santo, 100–101
  gasoline availability, 90–91
  insurance, 88
  safe traveling in, 87–96
  travel tips, 94–96
  vehicle repairs in, 92–93
  weather, 89–90
Bamburg, Glenn, 59, 64
Bamburg, Maxine, 59, 64
Bank services, 111–114
  automatic teller machines, 113
  personal identification and, 112
Bannan, Jan Gumprecht, 70
Bar Harbor, Maine, 8
Barjak, Emil, 97
Barnes, Patricia L., 24
Batteries
  cold-cranking amp rating, 156
  construction, 154–155
  deep cycle, 155–156
  hybrid, 156
  inspecting, 151–153
  maintenance, 151–156
  maintenance-free, 156
  reserve capacity, 156
  safety tips, 152
  testing, 153–154
Bayfield Peninsula, Wisconsin, 38, 43
Beckley, West Virginia, 16–17
Blarney, Ireland, 104
Blue Hill Peninsula, Maine, 9
Bluestone Lake, West Virginia, 15
Bluestone River, West Virginia, 15
Bluestone State Park, West Virginia, 15
Boston, Massachusetts, 20–22
Brake fluid, 158
Brakes
  drums, inspecting, 159–160
  hoses and lines, 161
  inspection of, 157–162
  master cylinder, 157–158
  operating principles, 162
  pads and linings, 160, 162
  parking, 162
  power booster systems, 158
  rotors, inspecting, 159
  tag-axle, 161
  temperature between frictional surfaces, 160, 162
Bridge of the Gods (Oregon/Washington), 71
Brown County State Park, Louisiana, 47
Bucksport, Maine, 9
Burkhart, C. J., 121
Burris, Dora, 53
Burris, Fred, 53
Buttermilk Falls State Park, New York, 27

Cabo San Lucas, Mexico, 85
Cadillac Mountain, Maine, 8
California. *See* Joshua Tree National Monument
Campobello International Park, New Brunswick, Canada, 9–10
Cascade Locks National Historic Site, Oregon, 70–71
Cascade Locks, Oregon, 75
Castine, Maine, 9
Chama, New Mexico, 121, 124
Charles River, Massachusetts, 21–22
Checks, personal, 114
Chimayo, New Mexico, 147

Cobb, Mary, 11
Colorado
  narrow-gauge steam trains, 121–127
  San Juan Mountains, 146–147
Colorado Desert, California, 76
Colorado River, 64, 68, 146
Colter, John, 61–62
Columbia Gorge (stern-wheeler), 70–71
Columbia River Gorge, Oregon, 70–75
Columbia River Scenic Highway, Oregon, 74
Constitutional Bicentennial, 171–175, 176, 179
Continental Divide, 54
Coolant, 165
Cooling system
  capacity, 165
  cleaning, 167
  function, 167–168
  maintenance, 163–168
  operating principles, 167
  pressure-testing, 163, 165
Cork, Ireland, 104
Cork (county), Ireland, 102
Cottonwood Springs, California, 77
Courtney, Gerald F., 19
Courtney, Myrna L., 19
Credit cards, 111, 112, 114
Creole Nature Trail, Louisiana, 30–35
Cumbres & Toltec Scenic Railroad (C&TS), 121, 124, 127

Dead Horse Point State Park, Utah, 68–69
Delaware, 184–188
Denver and Rio Grande Railway Company (D&RG), 123–124
Desert Christ Park, Yucca Valley, California, 81
Desert flora and fauna, 76–80
Dingle Peninsula, Ireland, 106–107
Drive belts, 165–166
Duluth, Minnesota, 38–39, 42
Du Pont mansion, Delaware, 185–187
Durango, Colorado, 121
Durango & Silverton Narrow Gauge Railroad (D&SNG), 121–126

Egrets, 32–33, 35
Electronic fund-transfer agreements, 114
Ellsworth, Maine, 8
Emerson, Doug, 76
Engine, operating temperature of, 166
Espíritu Santo, Mexico, 100–101
Evansville, Indiana, 48
Exum School of Mountaineering, 60

Fan belts, 163–164
Finger Lakes, New York, 24–27
Fishing, 134–139
Flea markets and swap meets, 115–120
  costs, 118
  getting started, 116–118
  locations, 118–120
  major markets, 118–119
  sales techniques, 120
Fort Knox, Maine, 9
Fort Savannah Inn (Lewisburg, West Virginia), 17–18

General Lewis Inn (Lewisburg, West Virginia), 17
Gentryville, Indiana, 48
Glacier National Park, Montana, 52–56, 145–146
Good Sam Club, Mail Forwarding Service, 112
Gooseberry Falls State Park, Minnesota, 42
Gould, Dick, 111
Grand Isle State Park, Louisiana, 34
Grand Teton National Park, Wyoming, 58–63, 146
Greenbrier, The (White Sulphur Springs, West Virginia), 17, 18
Greenbrier River, West Virginia, 15
Grouse, 135

Hackberry, Louisiana, 1, 34
Handcraft Centers of New England, 20
Harmony Society, 47–48
Harvest Queen (stern-wheeler), 71–72
Hawthorne, Nathaniel, 23
Hinton, West Virginia, 15
Hintz, Martin, 44
Hoctor, Fred, 84
Hood River Marina Park, Oregon, 75
Hoosier National Forest, Indiana, 47
Houston River, Louisiana, 30
Huggler, Tom, 131
Hydrometers
  antifreeze, 165–166
  for battery-checking, 155

Idaho. *See* Sawtooth Mountains
Identification, personal, 112
Indiana, 44–49
Indianapolis, Indiana, 48–49
Insurance, Mexican, 88
Ireland, southwestern, 102–107
Ithaca, New York, 27

Jenny Lake, Grand Teton National Park, 60, 62
Joshua Tree National Monument, California, 76–81

Kerry (county), Ireland, 102–103, 106

Killarney, Ireland, 106
Kinsale, Ireland, 105

Lafayette, Indiana, 46
Lake Fausse State Park, Louisiana, 34
Lake Powell, 147–148
La Paz, Mexico, 100
La Sal Mountains, Utah, 69
Lake Superior, 38–43
Leigh Lake, Grand Teton National Park, 60
Leonard, Barbara, 115, 171
Lewis, Peter M., 30
Lewisburg, West Virginia, 17–18
Lincoln, Abraham, 48
Lincoln Boyhood Home National Memorial, Lincoln City, Indiana, 48
Louisiana. *See* Creole Nature Trail
Lubec, Maine, 10

McBride, Sherry, 113
McIlhenny, Edward Avery, 35
Mail, receiving on road, 112–113
Maine. *See* Acadia National Park
Maintenance
  of batteries, 151–156
  of brakes, 157–162
  of cooling system, 163–168
Mammoth Hot Springs, Yellowstone National Park, 63
Manti-La Sal National Forest, Utah, 69
Martin, Antone, 81
Massachusetts, 19–23
Master cylinder, 157–158
Mayflower II (stern-wheeler), 22
Mazatlan, Mexico, 100
Mexico. *See* Baja California, Mexico
Minnesota. *See* Duluth, Minnesota
Moab, Utah, 64, 67, 69, 146
Mohave Desert, California, 76
Money orders, 114
Mormons, 64
Mount Desert Island, Maine, 5–10
Multnomah Falls, Oregon, 74–75

Nashville, Indiana, 47
National Memorial Arch, Valley Forge, Pennsylvania, 182, 183
New Brunswick, Canada, 9–10
New Castle, Delaware, 187–188
New Harmony, Indiana, 47–48
New Iberia, Louisiana, 34, 35
New Mexico, 147
  narrow-gauge steam trains, 121, 124
  quail-hunting, 132–133
New River, West Virginia, 15–16
New River Gorge Bridge, West Virginia, 16
New York. *See* Finger Lakes

Old Faithful, Yellowstone National Park, 62–63
Oneonta Gorge, Oregon, 75
Oregon. *See* Columbia River Gorge
Orlando, Florida, 172
Osier, Colorado, 127
Overheating, and cooling system maintenance, 166–167, 168
Owen, Robert, 48

Paria Canyon Primitive Area, 148
Pennsylvania. *See* Philadelphia; Valley Forge
Penobscot River, Maine, 9
Philadelphia, Pennsylvania, 171, 172, 175, 176–180
Pipestem Resort State Park, West Virginia, 11–15, 17, 18
Plimouth Plantation, Plymouth, Massachusetts, 22
Plymouth Rock, 22
Pokagon State Park, Indiana, 46
Portsmouth, Virginia, 175
Poss, Bill, 140
Postal services, 112

Quail-hunting, 131–135

Radiator
  core, maintenance of, 164, 165
  size, and effectiveness, 168
Railroads. *See* Steam trains, narrow-gauge
Rapp, George, 47
Ring of Kerry, Ireland, 106
Robert Treman State Park, New York, 24, 26–27
Robertson, Brian, 151, 157, 163
Rockefeller Wildlife Refuge, Louisiana, 34
Rocky Mountains. *See* Glacier National Park
Roosevelt, Eleanor, 10
Roosevelt, Franklin Delano, 9–10

Sabine National Wildlife Refuge, Louisiana, 31
Salem, Indiana, 45
Salem, Massachusetts, 22–23
Salmon River, Idaho, 144
Sam Houston Jones State Park, Louisiana, 30–31, 32–33, 34
San Felipe, Mexico, 85
San Juan Mountains, Colorado, 146–147
Sawtooth Mountains, Idaho, 144–145
Sea of Cortez, Mexico, 85
  Espíritu Santo (island), 97–101
Sedona, Arizona, 147
Silverton, Colorado, 121, 147
Smith, Geraldine R., 38, 181
Smith, Robert J., 5, 38, 176, 181
Snake River, 60, 146
Steam trains, narrow-gauge, 121–127
Stern-wheelers, 70–71, 74, 75

Sturbridge Village, Sturbridge, Massachusetts, 22
Superior, Lake. *See* Lake Superior
Superior, Wisconsin, 38, 43
Swap meets. *See* Flea markets and swap meets

Taos, New Mexico, 147
Taughannock Falls State Park, New York, 25, 27
Telephone answering machines, 112
Telluride, Colorado, 147
Teton Range, 58–63, 146
Thermostats, 166
Tippecanoe Battlefield State Memorial, Indiana, 46
Trains. *See* Steam trains, narrow-gauge
Traveler's checks, 114
Treman Lake, New York, 27
Trust agreements, 113
Twentynine Palms, California, 80

Utah, southeastern, 64–69, 146

Valley Forge, Pennsylvania, 181–183

Washington, George, 181–182
Washington, D.C., 172
Water pump, 167
West Virginia, 11–18
Wheel cylinders, 161
White River State Park, Indiana, 49
White Sulphur Springs, West Virginia, 17
Wildlife refuges, 34
Wilmington, Delaware, 184–185
Wilmington & Western Railroad, 185
Wolfe, John, 67
Wolfe Ranch, Utah, 67, 68
Women's Forum State Park, Oregon, 74
Wood, Jerry, 134–139
Wyoming. *See* Grand Teton National Park; Yellowstone National Park

Yellowstone National Park, Wyoming, 62–63, 146
Yucca Valley, California, 81

Zion National Park, Utah, 148
Zumbo, Jim, 134